THE CARIBBEAN WORLD AND THE UNITED STATES

Mixing Rum and Coca-Cola

Twayne's International History Series

Akira Iriye, editor
Harvard University

THE CARIBBEAN WORLD AND THE UNITED STATES

Mixing Rum and Coca-Cola

Robert Freeman Smith
University of Toledo

TWAYNE PUBLISHERS • NEW YORK
MAXWELL MACMILLAN CANADA • TORONTO
MAXWELL MACMILLAN INTERNATIONAL • NEW YORK OXFORD SINGAPORE SYDNEY

#29258784

Twayne Publishers
Macmillan Publishing Company
866 Third Avenue
New York, New York 10022

Maxwell Macmillan Canada, Inc.
1200 Eglinton Avenue East
Suite 200
Don Mills, Ontario M3C 3N1

Printed in the United States of America.

Library of Congress Cataloging-in-Publication Data
Smith, Robert Freeman, 1930–
The Caribbean World and the United States / Robert Freeman Smith.
p. cm. — (Twayne's international history series ; 11)
Includes bibliographical references and index.
ISBN 0-8057-7925-6 — ISBN 0-8057-9220-1 (pbk.)
1. Caribbean area—Foreign relations—United States. 2. United States—Foreign relations—Caribbean area. 3. United States—Foreign relations—1945–. 4. Caribbean area—Foreign relations—1945–. I. Title.
F2178.U6S65 1994
327.729073—dc20   93-33912
                                                         CIP

The paper used in this publication meets the minimum requirements of American National Standard for Information Sciences—Permanence of Paper for Printed Library Materials. ANSI Z39.48-1984.

10 9 8 7 6 5 4 3 2 1 (alk. paper)

10 9 8 7 6 5 4 3 2 1 (pbk.: alk. paper)

To Charlotte, my wife, for the
strength and inspiration to take up
the pen once more; and to
Cuddles, the furry dog who slept
under my desk like another dog
named Peggy at another time, for
another book

CONTENTS

ILLUSTRATIONS

FOREWORD

Twayne's International History Series seeks to publish reliable and readable accounts of post–World War II international affairs. Today, nearly 50 years after the end of the war, the time seems opportune to undertake a critical assessment of world affairs in the second half of the twentieth century. What themes and trends have characterized international relations since 1945? How have they evolved and changed? What connections have developed between international and domestic affairs? How have states and peoples defined and pursued their objectives and what have they contributed to the world at large? How have conceptions of warfare and visions of peace changed?

These questions must be addressed if one is to arrive at an understanding of the contemporary world that is both international—with an awareness of the linkages among different parts of the world—and historical—with a keen sense of what the immediate past has brought to human civilization. Hence Twayne's International History Series. It is to be hoped that the volumes in this series will help the reader to explore important events and decisions since 1945 and to develop a global awareness and historical sensitivity with which to confront today's problems.

The first volumes in the series examine the United States' relations with other countries, groups of countries, or regions. The focus on the United States is justified in part because of the nation's predominant positions in postwar international relations, and also because far more extensive documentation is available on American foreign affairs than is the case with other countries. The series addresses not only those interested in international relations but also those studying America's and other countries' histories, who will find here useful guides and fresh insights into the recent past. Now more than ever it is imperative to understand the complex ties between national and international history.

In this volume Robert Freeman Smith, the author of a number of important studies of U.S. relations with Mexico and other countries in the Western

Hemisphere, presents a fascinating story of the Caribbean, its people, their culture, and the United States' military, economic, and cultural involvement in the Caribbean peoples' affairs. Readers who have perused the author's earlier writings may be struck that he is less critical of U.S. policies and strategies in this volume than elsewhere. Those who have read John H. Coatsworth's book in the series, *Central America and the United States*, will also note a very different approach to the region. I welcome the presentation of different interpretations and perspectives, for by comparing and examining sharply divergent views of the past, one gains fresh insights not only into international history but into the writing of that history as well.

Akira Iriye

PREFACE

Ask most Americans what they think or know about the Caribbean and you will probably get a catalog of things such as Bacardi rum, Piña Colladas, bannana daiquiris, Macanudo cigars, calypso music, and cha cha cha. And some would include a list of famous personalities like Harry Bellafonte, Desi Arnez, Geraldo Rivera, Roberto Clemente, and José Canseco. Others might mention sunny beaches in January, snorkeling, gambling casinos, and grilled conch. Perhaps a few place names might show up—San Juan Hill for history buffs, Guantananmo Bay for those who have sailed with the Caribbean fleet, and Charlotte Amalie for the duty-free shoppers.

The makers and shapers of American foreign policy would present another kind of analysis. For example, in 1931 Secretary of State Henry L. Stimson succinctly stated the basic importance of the Caribbean region to the United States:

> That locality has been the one spot external to our shores which nature has decreed to be most vital to our national safety, not to mention our prosperity. It commands the line of the great trade route which joins our eastern and western coasts. . . . Since the Panama Canal has become an accomplished fact, it has not only become the vital artery of our coastwise commerce but, as well, the link in our national defense which protects the defensive power of our fleet. One cannot fairly appraise American policy toward Latin America . . . without taking into consideration all of the elements of which it is the resultant.[1]

Stimson stressed the interests that have made the Caribbean one of the most important international areas to the United States even from the beginning of the nation's history. And this interest predates independence by at least a century.

Almost a century before Secretary Stimson wrote these words, Secretary of State John Quincy Adams wrote concerning Cuba and Puerto Rico, "These islands, from their local position, are natural appendages to the North American continent; and one of them, Cuba, almost in sight of our shores, from a multitude of considerations has become an object of transcendent importance to the political and commercial interests of our Union." After listing several of these, including "its commanding position with reference to the Gulf of Mexico and the West India seas," Adams stated that all of these factors, "give it an importance in the sum of our national interests, with which that of no other foreign territory can be compared, and little inferior to that which binds the different members of this Union together."[2]

This list of quotations could be expanded ad infinitum, but the point should be clear—the Caribbean is central to the historical definition of U.S. national interests. Over the course of its history the United States has been more consistently involved in the Caribbean than any other area in the world. This should not be surprising, as the Caribbean forms part of the southern frontier of the United States. Until the twentieth century the area was virtually a European-controlled lake. Spain, France, Great Britain, the Netherlands, Denmark, and even Sweden had colonies in the Caribbean, and it was not until 1898 that the United States really began to challenge this European domination.

The Caribbean has been of major importance for several reasons. The great inland water transportation system flowing from the Ohio, the Tennessee, the Arkansas, and other rivers into the Mississippi in effect makes the American heartland a part of the Caribbean arena. The water transportation routes both from the Gulf ports and through the Panama Canal are of major significance for security and economic reasons. In the latter part of the twentieth century some 45 percent of all U.S. imports and exports, 55 percent of crude oil imports, and 60 percent of supplies for the North Atlantic Treaty Organization pass through the Caribbean. In addition, 65 percent of all ships transiting the Panama Canal carry goods to or from the United States. In short, the nation that controls the Caribbean controls the United States.

The trade connection predates the American Revolution and has developed into an important element in the economies of many of the Caribbean islands as well as the United States. The United States now imports a wide variety of products assembled in the area, such as baseballs, electronic goods, and clothing. In addition, traditional agricultural products such as bananas and sugar still constitute important elements in U.S.-Caribbean commerce. The area receives a variety of things from the United States, including thousands of tourists—a temporary but profitable import. American investments have played a significant role in economic development, perhaps more for the islands and some companies than for the U.S. economy overall. The massive Cuban nationalization of American companies did not have much effect on the economic well-being of the United States. Some U.S. companies have developed significant branch factories in places like Puerto Rico and the Dominican Republic, and under the auspices of the Caribbean Basin Initiative the economies of the Caribbean and the United States will probably continue to become more integrated.

The Caribbean involvement of the United States has tended to receive harsh treatment from some academic critics, usually of the liberal-left persuasion. In their eyes the United States has not transformed the region into some kind of paradise and has "perverted" its development by somehow forcing it into a mold that only benefits the United States. Without the United States, the Caribbean would be much poorer in all respects.

Have the policies of the United States been successful? In the long run I think that the answer is yes. Anthony Lake, who served in the State Department in the 1970s, has written that almost all foreign policies are compromises and not the product of some "grand strategic design." As a result, "Success in foreign policy is seldom absolute triumph. It is usually the achievement of modest progress, or the avoidance of disaster."[3] This is a reasonable conclusion for the Caribbean. The region is generally free from foreign control and influence, and the type that remains is quite benevolent and voluntary. The Cayman Islands, for example, contentedly remain part of the British Commonwealth. The Caribbean area has more freedom, democracy, and general respect for human rights (with the exception of Cuba and Haiti) than at any time since the Spanish Conquest. And the pre-Conquest, Caribbean world was no Garden of Eden.

Some argue that the United States has relied too much on military force. Certainly armed intervention has been a factor in U.S. policy, but it has been an off and on type of involvement that has always been characterized by the voluntary withdrawal of U.S. forces—usually after a fairly short period of time. Sometimes the military has been intelligently used and sometimes not. It is a mixed picture. Some military interventions have solved nothing, others have accomplished a great deal. Eternal peace has not come to the area, and never will, but there is a reasonable amount of stability and peace in the area. Thomas Paine best characterized the overall U.S. approach when he wrote, "I am thus far a Quaker that I would gladly agree with all the world to lay aside the use of arms and settle matters by negotiations; but unless the whole world will, the matter ends, and I take up my musket and THANK HEAVEN He has put it on my power." And so to the story at hand.[4]

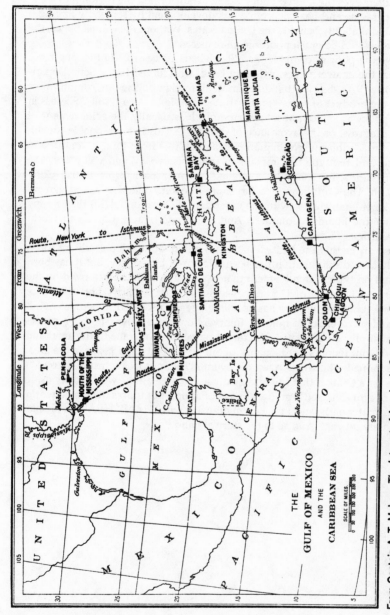

THE
GULF OF MEXICO
AND THE
CARIBBEAN SEA

SCALE OF MILES
0 50 100 150 200 250 300

From Captain A. T. Mahan, *The Interest of America in Sea Power: Present and Future* (1898), 269–70.

chapter 1

CARIBBEAN INTERESTS
AND U.S. POLICY TO 1945

It was the height of the fever season in July 1741 when the British navy, under the command of Vice Admiral Edward Vernon, reached the coast of Cuba. Vernon's objective was the port and capital city of St. Iago (later Santiago); the setting was the War of Jenkin's Ear (the British Parliament used the loss of smuggler Robert Jenkin's ear, in an engagement with the Spanish navy off the Florida coast, as a pretext to declare war on Spain), which was another chapter in the struggle between Great Britain, France, and Spain—the latter two nations usually allies—to establish colonies in the Western Hemisphere. The Caribbean had become one of the major arenas of conflict in this war that was waged intermittently for over a century.

The British Colonies in North America became enmeshed in this strategic conflict, and some 3,600 colonials from North America were part of Admiral Vernon's force. Governor Gooch of Virginia praised the expedition as a "holy war against Spanish power in the West Indies," and a colonial officer named Lawrence Washington was so proud of his service with the admiral that on his return he named his Potomac River estate Mount Vernon—his younger brother, George, would later inherit it. But the expedition was a total failure, and out of some 1,500 volunteers from New England only 150 returned. The rest died of tropical diseases.[1]

Yet in 1762, during the French and Indian War, the British once more asked for colonial volunteers. By obscuring the destination of the new expedition, the British obtained 4,000 men from four colonies, who joined Admiral George Pocock's force of 11,000 regulars and 40 warships. In June 1762 they were part of the assault on Havana, Cuba. The Spaniards surrendered on 11

1

August, and there were only seven American casualties. When the expedition departed in October, however, almost half the Americans had died of tropical diseases.[2]

By 1776 the Caribbean had become identified in the minds of North Americans as an area of strategic/military interest and a source of potential military threat because the region was virtually a European-controlled lake. Thus Americans had become part of the Caribbean power struggle even before gaining their independence.

In like manner, British North America developed extensive economic ties with the West Indies. As early as 1662 New Englanders were cutting logwood trees on the coast of Yucatán and the Bay of Campeche. By 1715 Boston merchants dominated the logwood trade. Despite opposition from British authorities, merchant shippers from New York, New England, Pennsylvania, and Baltimore steadily increased their trade in the Caribbean. After the British occupation of Havana, some 1,067 ships from New York alone entered Havana harbor in 1763. By 1775 close to 40 percent of all ships leaving the ports of New York and Boston sailed directly to the British West Indies. In 1767 some 2,000 vessels cleared through American ports for all parts of the West Indies.

By the mid-eighteenth century Caribbean trade played an important role in the prosperity of British North America, providing one of the few sources of hard currency for the colonials. This trade increasingly strained the limits of mercantilistic regulation, however—especially for New England's trade in slaves, molasses, sugar, and rum. The Spanish and French West Indies became a cheaper source of molasses for the some 150 rum distilleries of New England. When Britain from 1763 onward tried to force the Colonies to abide by the Navigation Acts and to confine their trade to the British Empire, the colonists started the conflict that led to war and independence. Before 1776 Caribbean trade had been established as an important element in the interests of North Americans.

The Caribbean also played an important role during the War of Independence. Santo Domingo served as a supply base for shipments of arms and munitions to the Continental Army even before the Franco-American treaty of 1778. The same island also served as the base of operations for the French fleet that helped trap General Cornwallis's army at Yorktown in 1781. Spain opened its Cuban ports to trade with North Americans in 1778 and used these as bases to attack the British in Florida.

From its beginning the government of the United States saw the Caribbean as important to its national interests. John Adams wrote to Robert Livingston in 1783 that "our natural share in the West India trade is all that is now wanting to complete the plan of happiness and prosperity of our country. Deprived of it we shall be straitened and shackeled in some degree. We cannot enjoy a free use of all our limbs without this; with it I see nothing to desire, nothing to vex or chagrin our people, nothing to interrupt our repose or keep up a dread of war."[3]

Unfortunately, Adams saw his hopes and expectations shattered after the war. The British closed their West Indies colonies to American ships, and even the former ally Spain closed the ports of Cuba in May 1783, seized the goods of two ships belonging to the new U.S. commercial agent, Oliver Pollock, and finally expelled all foreigners in 1785. Of course Americans could trade with the French Indies under the Commercial Treaty of 1778, but in reality the treaty was almost worthless. Both nations had extended most-favored-nation (MFN) treatment to the other. In practice, French traders had almost the same rights in the United States as U.S. citizens, since the country had no restrictions on trade. On the other hand, the French placed numerous and highly restrictive controls on trade in general, so the MFN principle only granted Americans equal discrimination.

The closing of the Caribbean trade was an important factor in the postwar depression that plagued the American economy. Attempts to negotiate trade agreements generally failed, owing to the federal government's lack of power to force the states to abide by terms of any agreement, and this provided an important drive for a stronger central government. After the new government was established under the Constitution, an attempt was made to open trade with the British West Indies in the Jay Treaty of 1794, but the Senate rejected the clause providing for a very limited access by U.S. ships and a prohibition on exports of certain agricultural products from the United States. The issue of trade with the Caribbean colonies would remain unresolved until after the War of 1812.

The French Revolution in 1789 and the rise of Napoleon Bonaparte led to war between the European powers that continued off and on until 1815. This conflict had significant economic and military consequences for the Caribbean. Cuba became increasingly dependent on imports from the United States after 1793, owing to Spain's involvement in the war. In like fashion, American merchants began to enjoy a most profitable relationship with other West Indian colonies, even without benefit of treaty. Between 1790 and 1814 Caribbean commerce took more than one-third of all U.S. exports.

The French Revolution erupted in the western, or French, part of Santo Domingo (later called Haiti) during the 1790s as both the free blacks and slaves struggled for power. As the black slaves fought for their freedom, thousands of French planters fled. Some came to the southern United States with stories of pillage and bloodshed that would influence subsequent U.S. attitudes toward independence movements in the Caribbean.

As the European conflict spilled over into the Caribbean, the United States' interests were affected. Both the French and British navies stopped U.S. merchant ships and seized "contraband" goods. The French, however, proved the most aggressive: by 1798 70 percent of all U.S. losses of goods in the Caribbean were inflicted by the French navy. An undeclared naval war with France erupted in the Caribbean, and the U.S. and British navies began a policy of cooperation. This involved exchange of signals, the use of bases, convoying, and a common policy toward Toussaint L'Ouverture, the leader of the revolutionary forces in Haiti. The U.S. Navy began to operate out of such bases as Prince Rupert Bay (Dominica) and Basseterre Roads (St. Christopher, or St. Kitts), sending thousands of French prisoners to the jail in Basseterre.[4]

The U.S. government had been very ambivalent about the establishment of a black republic in Haiti, but strategic factors briefly overcame this dilemma. After Britain ended its efforts to control the island, a diplomatic accord between Britain, the United States, and Toussaint L'Ouverture was worked out by 1799, and President John Adams lifted the embargo on American trade with the island. When Toussaint's army faltered in the civil war with his rival André Rigaud, Toussaint appealed to Britain and the U.S. for direct support. The commander of the British forces did not cooperate and in fact seized ships carrying supplies to Toussaint. The U.S. Navy fulfilled the U.S. commitment, sending its squadron at Cap-François to Toussaint's aid. The USS *General Greene* blockaded Jacmel and in February 1800 supported the attack by Toussaint's army with naval gunfire. Other American ships carried supplies to his forces in the southern part of the island. Thus Toussaint won control with the support of the United States. Meanwhile, the infant U.S. Navy won its first victories when Commodore Thomas Truxton commanding the USS *Constitution* smashed the French naval vessels *Insurgente* in February 1799 and *La Vengeance* a year later.[5]

President John Adams signed a treaty with France in September 1800 that terminated the undeclared naval war and the alliance of 1778. He then ordered U.S. forces to cease aiding Toussaint. Peace with France was considered by Adams to be more important than the creation of a black republic in the Caribbean. Yet, in a paradoxical and unintended way, Haiti came to the aid of the United States. Napoleon Bonaparte decided to reassert French control over the island in order to utilize sugar revenue to build French military forces. To supply the colony with food, he also forced Spain to give back the Louisiana Territory in North America. When President Thomas Jefferson heard about the secret cession, he wrote to the U.S. minister to France that the day France took possession of New Orleans, "we must marry ourselves to the British fleet and nation."[6] And, Minister Robert Livingston was authorized to try to buy New Orleans.

Napoleon, however, offered to sell the entire Louisiana Territory. What had happened? The Haitian rebels and tropical diseases had decimated the French army. Napoleon's brother-in-law, Marshall Victor Leclerc, died of yellow fever, and by early 1803 some 50,000 French soldiers had perished. Napoleon's prestige received a severe blow, and he decided that victory in Haiti was not worth the price. So, in withdrawing from that island he no longer needed Louisiana. Besides, he could use the $15 million in gold that the U.S. ended up borrowing from the British House of Baring.

Thus the former slaves of Haiti helped to pave the way for the largest, peaceful, territorial acquisition in American history. In 1804 Haiti became the second independent republic in the Western Hemisphere, but the United States would not extend diplomatic recognition to Haiti for another 58 years.

In 1815 a nationalistic United States once more resumed efforts to open the Caribbean to U.S. commerce through establishment of the principle of reciprocity of trade and commercial regulations. Congress used retaliation against the British in the Navigation Acts of 1818 and 1820. The first closed all American ports to British ships that came from ports closed to the United

States; the second applied the closing to British ships coming from any colonial port in America and prohibited the importation of goods from British colonial ports—even in American ships—unless the goods came directly from the producing colony. The latter provision was designed to block the circuitous trade through Bermuda, Nova Scotia, and New Brunswick. The British Parliament offered a liberalization of the West Indies trade in 1822, and the United States relaxed its restrictions by presidential proclamation and by an act of Congress in March 1823. President John Quincy Adams did not respond to subsequent British offers of relaxation, but President Andrew Jackson accepted these in 1830. As a result, reciprocal trade relations between the United States and the British West Indies was established. Negotiations with Sweden and France concerning their West Indian colonies led to reciprocal agreements with those countries in 1837 and 1828, respectively. The Spanish colonies of Cuba and Puerto Rico had been closed officially, but the regulations were not enforced. In 1830 Spain accepted a U.S. consul for Cuba, and trade between the United States and Cuba increased.

In the decade after the War of 1812 the U.S. Navy launched an all-out attack on piracy in the Caribbean, thus beginning the function of area policeman—or "gunboat diplomacy"—that the United States would increasingly assume during the century. According to established international practice of the nineteenth century, respectable nations had to be able to protect the lives and property of their citizens abroad and enforce what were regarded as civilized standards of international behavior. Gunboat diplomacy was considered to be necessary, normal, and legal, and it was carried out in those parts of the world where the navy was the only representative of the national government. The U.S. Navy established its West Indies squadron in 1821, and Commodore David Porter worked out with the British navy an arrangement whereby captured pirates were taken to Jamaica, tried by an Admiralty Court, and hanged from the yardarm. This solved the problem created by jury trials in New Orleans, where the pirates' peers usually released them. Porter also pioneered in the use of steam power by the navy when he added a former Hudson River steamboat to his command in 1823. The USS *Seagull* mounted three guns and could chase pirate ships close to shore and up island rivers. By the 1830s the Caribbean was a much more peaceful and safe area.

The turmoil produced by the independence movements in Latin America made Cuba a focal point for conflict between France, Britain, and the United States. Some Creole planters in Cuba were interested in being annexed by the United States because Cuban liberals were advocating autonomy and the abolition of slavery. Advances were made to the United States in 1811 and revived in 1822. U.S. opinion about annexation was mixed: few if any of those in favor were willing to go to war to win Cuba, and the major problem became one of keeping Cuba free from British or French control. Such influential Americans as John Quincy Adams and Jefferson feared French interference and the possibility that Britain would demand Cuba as its price for supporting Spain against France. Both men believed that Cuba would eventually become part of the United States because it was, in Adams's words a "natural appendage to the North American continent."[7]

During the 1820s most American leaders agreed that in the short run the most feasible policy was for weak Spain to retain the island. On several occasions the United States sought support from various European countries for its No-Transfer policy. In 1823 the British foreign secretary proposed a mutual "self-denying" pledge in regard to Cuba and Mexico as part of a joint declaration against European (namely French) interference in Latin America. Secretary of State Adams did not want to enter into any agreement that would prevent the United States from annexing Cuba in the future. His views prevailed, and President James Monroe delivered a unilateral statement of American policy in December 1823. Cuba was not the only, or even the major, factor behind what became known as the Monroe Doctrine. The struggle for influence in the Caribbean and Central American area was an important factor, and Cuba continued to be a focal point in this struggle.

After 1826, with the major competing powers in tacit agreement over Spanish control of Cuba, a period of relative calm ensued. After 1830 Americans went to Cuba to invest in the sugar industry and brought their technology of steam engines and railroads with them. Trade between Cuba and the United States increased as the latter became a much more vital factor in the island's economy.

From the early 1820s to the mid-1840s the U.S. government rather consistently supported Spanish control of Cuba and cooperated with Spain against Cuban internal revolts. In this respect the administrations of Adams, Jackson, Martin Van Buren, and John Tyler followed the same policy toward Cuba. The situation changed in the 1840s, when the Democratic party became the aggressive advocate of territorial expansion. Stimulated by a variety of factors that appealed to interests in all sections, the Democrats renewed the drive for territory that resulted in the push to the Pacific. With this accomplished, President James K. Polk turned to Cuba in 1848.

As a result of the Mexican War, which ended in 1848, the United States acquired ports on the Pacific coast. Suddenly, the Caribbean assumed even greater importance as it became an essential link in potential transportation routes from the east coast to the west coast. To sail from New York to California around the tip of South America took 76 days and was somewhat hazardous, especially in the Straits of Magellan. In the era before transcontinental railroads the overland trip consumed almost a month of travel by railroad from New York to St. Joseph, Missouri, and stagecoach from there to San Francisco. And the freight rates were extremely high for overland commerce. Thus the Caribbean became part of a shorter, cheaper shipping route that crossed the isthmus at Panama. With the completion of a rail line across the isthmus in 1855, travel time was cut to about 30 days.[8]

An indication of the growing importance of the Caribbean and the trans-isthmian shipping route to the United States came in 1846, when the Polk administration negotiated the Bidlack-Mallarino Treaty (or Treaty of New Grenada) with New Grenada (Colombia). The latter country wanted the United States to protect the isthmus of Panama, and the United States agreed to maintain freedom of transit across the isthmus and to guarantee the sovereignty of New Grenada over Panama. In the Clayton-Bulwer Treaty of 1850, the United States and Great Britain agreed to joint control of any future isthmian canal and a pledge that neither country would "occupy," "colonize," or exercise "dominion" over any part of Central America. Not all of the problems involving the United States and Britain in Central America were resolved, but basically the major potential threat to this strategic American shipping route had been taken care of.

The growing entanglement of territorial expansion with sectional antagonisms, however, acted to reduce the aggressiveness of the U.S. push into the Caribbean. The Polk administration offered Spain $100 million for Cuba but made no threat to use force to take it. The northern states were becoming increasingly critical toward the addition of new slave states, and some northerners called the Mexican War "The Great Slave Power Conspiracy." Thus any talk of moving into the Caribbean automatically produced charges that the South was again trying to push the country into war. The Whig administration of Zachary Taylor that assumed control of the executive branch in 1849 withdrew the purchase offer and generally reverted to the policy of the 1820s and 1830s in regard to Spanish control of Cuba.

In 1848 General Narciso López—a Venezuelan who had served in the Spanish army and as an official in Cuba—emerged as the leader of a renewed drive for revolt against Spanish rule of Cuba. Many Cubans in this movement also wanted Cuba to be annexed by the United States. The Cuban Council in New York City declared for annexation in 1849, and Cubans in the same city published an annexationist newspaper—La Verdad—from 1848 to 1853.

Although the U.S. government tried to enforce the neutrality laws, Lopez managed to launch two expeditions against Cuba. The first, in 1850, set out from New Orleans with some 750 men. One ship made it to Cuba, but Lopez and his followers had to race back to the United States when the expected uprising did not materialize. The other two ships were captured, but the men were later pardoned by the Queen of Spain. Lopez was arrested and brought to trial for violation of the neutrality laws, but a sympathetic southern jury would not convict him. In 1851 Lopez sailed from New Orleans with about 400 men. He was again captured and this time garroted in the Havana public square. Some of his followers were shot, and about 160 others were sent to prison in Spain. These prisoners pleaded for diplomatic intercession on the grounds that they had been misled by Lopez; they were pardoned in 1852.

Franklin Pierce came to the presidency in 1853 determined to pursue an aggressive foreign policy as a device for soothing the festering sectional conflict. The administration, however, started out with a cautious approach to the Cuban problem. This changed early in 1854 when Spanish officials seized the American steamer Black Warrior off the coast of Cuba. This stirred up nationalistic protests against Spain and put new heat into the expansionists' desire for Cuba. In the South this ambition was further inflamed by renewed reports on British schemes to abolish slavery in Cuba and to set up an "Africanized" republic aimed at creating instability in the United States.

Secretary of State William L. Marcy instructed the minister to Spain, Pierre Soule, to renew the purchase offer, but he also hinted broadly that the United States would aid the Cubans in any efforts to overthrow Spanish control. This was a most welcome opportunity to Soule, a red-hot expansionist who had migrated to New Orleans from France. Soule had already broached the subject to Queen Isabella and was convinced that Spain would give up Cuba if the United States took an aggressive position. The minister, however, pushed the Cuban issue beyond the bounds of diplomatic propriety. He had gained a kind of notoriety by wounding the French ambassador in a duel, and he further displayed his impetuous nature by meddling in Spanish politics and by antagonizing the Spanish government.

The administration hoped to take advantage of the Crimean War and Spanish internal difficulties, but plans for appointing a special commission to negotiate with Spain were opposed by Congress. As an alternative the administration instructed Soule to confer with James Buchanan and John Mason, the ministers to England and France, respectively. The three were told to formulate recommendations, and the result was the Ostend Manifesto, which was signed at Aix-la-Chapelle. Soule thought that this report was too weak, and in a private letter to Marcy he advocated the use of force.

Pierce and Marcy, however, had retreated from the aggressive posture taken in April. Controversy surrounding the Kansas-Nebraska Act had erupted in the interim, and Soule's diplomacy, coupled with the Ostend Manifesto, further inflamed sectional feeling. Marcy in effect rebuked Soule and stated that the administration did not favor a coercive policy. Soule resigned, but the administration's northern opponents continued to hammer away at the Democrats as the party of aggressive "slavocracy."

Democratic president James Buchanan tried to purchase Cuba on several occasions between 1857 and 1860. He was vigorously supported in these efforts by the southern wing of the party, which saw Cuba as the southern arena for Manifest Destiny and the hope for new slave states in the union. This was the specific basis for the fight over the Wilmot Proviso's attempt to ban the further expansion of slavery into the territories in 1846. Of course northern Republicans and southern Democrats knew that cotton could not be grown in Nebraska or the Dakotas, hence the expansion of slavery into these areas was an impossibility. By 1850 they were arguing over Cuba because the Wilmot Proviso (the basic issue of the Republican party, which was founded in 1854) would be an issue if the United States acquired the island. In fact, President Abraham Lincoln cited the case of Cuba when he rejected compromise proposals early in 1861. In one sense Cuba played a role in the coming of the Civil War.

President Buchanan also believed that the United States should exercise a police role in the Caribbean and Central America to ensure that disorderly conditions did not threaten foreign nationals or the transit routes across the Caribbean Basin. He argued that the United States must perform this function or European powers would intervene, as they had already done in Mexico. His requests for authority to use the armed forces in such interventions were denied by Congress. Almost 50 years would pass before President Theodore

Roosevelt enshrined this assertion of America's police power in the Caribbean as a corollary to the Monroe Doctrine.

The Dominican Republic was created in 1844 on the eastern-Spanish part of Santo Domingo. Bankruptcy and civil war characterized the new nation, and Dominican rulers would periodically approach the United States, offering to cede a naval base, or the country, in return for cash. The first such treaty between the U.S. and the Dominican Republic failed in 1853 when Britain and France objected. In 1861 Spain reoccupied its former colony but departed in 1865, owing partly to U.S. objections at the end of the Civil War when the United States showed that it could use its massive military strength in other than a civil war. The French occupying Mexico got the same message and also departed.

Secretary of State William Seward was interested in a naval base at Samana Bay. Confederate blockade runners had used Caribbean bases, and Seward believed that U.S. bases in the area were necessary. President Ulysses S. Grant also believed that former slaves could be sent to the island to form an all-black state of the United States, thus avoiding white domination. The Dominican government was willing to cede the base and the rest of the country as well, but the U.S. Senate rejected the annexation treaty in 1870. In fact, the Senate refused to act on Seward's 1867 treaty to purchase the Danish West Indies (Virgin Islands) for $7.5 million, even after Denmark ratified the treaty and the residents of the islands voted overwhelmingly to become a U.S. colony. The Danes wanted the money and angrily denounced the U.S. Senate for its perfidy.

The first major Cuban revolt against Spanish control began in 1868. The repercussions of the Ten Years' War were soon felt by the United States, as American-owned properties in Cuba were attacked. The United States offered to mediate the conflict. The American proposal contained a veiled hint that the United States would recognize the belligerent rights of the rebels if Spain refused. The Cubans rejected the armistice terms offered by Spain, and the war continued. President Grant signed a proclamation recognizing Cuban belligerency, but Secretary of State Hamilton Fish suppressed the document, and the neutrality policy was maintained.

In effect, neutrality was difficult to enforce. The Cuban junta in New York received aid from American citizens, and numerous expeditions provided the rebels with arms, supplies, and volunteers. In October 1873 one of the main ships engaged in this activity, the *Virginius*, was captured by a Spanish gunboat and 53 passengers and crewmen were executed. The rest were saved by the timely intervention of a British naval vessel. Some Americans demanded war, and the administration alternated between caution and belligerency. The navy (or, rather, what there was of it not confined to port) was put on a war footing, and plans were made for an attack on Havana. Grant and Fish, however, were not anxious to fight, and at last a compromise agreement was reached. The *Virginius* was released and Spain paid $80,000 to the families of the executed men.

The war continued to have an adverse effect on American trade and investments on the island. Having rejected recognition of either Cuban belligerency or independence, the administration finally proposed a joint intervention plan to several European nations. The plan was rejected. There was little support in the United States for war or expansion so the neutrality policy was continued until the war ended in 1878.

During the 1880s and 1890s the competition for empire between the major European powers increased sharply. Africa was divided, and the race for the final division of Asia seemed to be under way. To many informed people, it appeared certain that the competition for control of the world's territory, resources, and markets had entered the final stage. In turn, this rivalry was enhanced by nationalistic versions of the civilizing and Christianizing missions of each nation. Closely related to, and exacerbated by, the imperial conception of power and prestige was an intensified perception of commercial rivalry even in noncolonial areas. Driven by a fear of dropping behind and being shut out in the race for markets, national leaders utilized governmental powers in a variety of ways designed to improve the marketing position of their country. Protectionism at home and special, unilateral economic arrangements abroad (especially commercial agreements that discriminated against third parties) characterized these efforts.

During the Venezuelan boundary controversy with Britain, the United States was in the throes of another policy debate: what to do about the insurrection in Cuba that had started in 1895. Some saw the situation only in local terms, but others placed the Cuban problem in the larger context of international rivalry and power politics. In general, this latter assortment of private citizens and officals believed that the world was being closed by expanding empires and that if the United States did not assert some kind of power role in the Caribbean and Asia it would find itself isolated. Such isolation would have severe military, political, economic, and ideological effects on the country. In effect, the United States would be at the mercy of the most powerful. The country could choose not to play in the game of international power politics, but it could not avoid the consequences of such a decision.

An important part of this game was ensuring peace, order, and stability in what were called the backward nations. In such areas the power that provided the police function was the one that exerted major influence. By the 1890s a number of prominent Americans had adopted this European view of international relations. They believed that if the nation wanted to be taken seriously and have its interests treated with respect by other powers, then it had to assert the police function to restore and maintain peace and order in those parts of the world considered to be especially vital to American interests. The Caribbean and Gulf of Mexico had long been considered to be part of the American security zone, as the region was the access route to the nation's soft underbelly and the Mississippi-Ohio rivers transportation system. Central America had been added to the zone as American leaders accepted the idea that the United States must build and control an isthmian canal. Such a canal

"Another Hold-up and the Monroe Doctrine Sleeps On." Cartoon by R. C. Bowman from the Minneapolis *Tribune*, 10 May 1897.

would be militarily and economically vital for any expanded American role in South America and Asia. In the modern world of steel and steam navies, it could mean the difference between isolation and access. If the United States failed to maintain peace and order in its own backyard, however, then it could not expect to effectively protect a canal and its access routes. Thus, the argument ran, the United States had to assert a policing role in the Caribbean–Central American region or some other power would. In the context of events in Africa and Asia, many American leaders believed the country had to act to preclude greater European influence or control.

This general point of view did not prescribe any particular policy for implementation. Americans were severely divided over the question of specific policies and especially over the use of military force. The debate was further complicated by the resurgence of an ideological element in the nation's heritage—that the United States had a destiny (sometimes called manifest) to redeem the world by spreading Anglo-American civilization, republican government, and Protestant Christianity. Many included under civilization the promotion of economic development, education, and sanitation.

All of these issues and arguments emerged during the debate over the United States' role in Cuba's war for independence. President William McKinley did not want war but had accepted the idea that the United States was ultimately responsible for law and order in the Caribbean. When Spain could not settle the war either by winning or withdrawing, McKinley asked the Congress for authority to step in and pacify Cuba. Public enthusiasm for such a move had already been sharpened by stories of Spanish atrocities and by the sinking of the USS *Maine* in Havana harbor (February 1898). The president asked Congress to grant him authority to carry out the international duty of the United States—the peace-keeping functions of all civilized powers: "to take measures to secure a full and final termination of hostilities between the Government of Spain and the people of Cuba, and to secure in the island the establishment of a stable government, capable of maintaining order and observing its international obligations, insuring peace and tranquility and the security of its citizens as well as our own."[9]

Some Congressmen wanted the authorization to recognize Cuban independence under the auspices of Cuba's provisional government. McKinley and his advisors did not believe that this "government-in-the-woods," as some called it, was a functional entity capable of governing Cuba in peacetime. They feared that an independent Cuba under this regime would become another Haiti or Dominican Republic and create more temptations for European intervention. If the United States brought peace to Cuba, McKinley believed that the nation had an obligation to prepare the island for self-government and protect it in its republican infancy. The president stated that he would veto any resolution recognizing the independence of Cuba. He did accept, however, the compromise Teller Amendment, which stated that the United States would not annex Cuba and would "leave the government and control of the island to its people" after pacification had been accomplished.

As a result of the war with Spain and the Treaty of Paris (1898), the United States took its first step toward establishing a sphere of interest in the

"Uncle Sam: 'Enough of this—get off.'" Cartoon from the New York *World*, 4 March 1898.

Caribbean. Puerto Rico became an American colony and passed into a kind of limbo—forgotten by American leaders except for occasional bouts of liberalization when the colonial status would be modified. Cuba, however, was the key to the Gulf-Caribbean, and the status of the island and the role of the United States in Cuban affairs would be debated for several decades. The results, like those of the broader debate over predominance in the Caribbean–Central American region, would be a mixture of policies and actions characterized by paradox and ambiguity—a kind of ambivalent imperialism continually modified by guilt, domestic politics, and the lack of a true colonial drive.

To U.S. leaders, pacification of Cuba meant establishing a republican government, providing economic stability, and creating the infrastructure for an orderly society. The U.S. Army landed at Daiquiri, Cuba, on 22 June 1898, and after a short struggle Spain surrendered. As a result, the United States created a military government that ran Cuba from 1898 to 1902 and this experiment in nation building would influence U.S. policies in the region for the first quarter of the twentieth century. General Leonard Wood became the second military governor of Cuba in December 1899, and under his and Secretary of War Elihu Root's direction, extensive programs of sanitation, school building, teacher training, disease control, prison and mental hospital reform, judicial-system reforms, and governmental-structure development were implemented. Wood believed that stable government and orderly society required "good schools, good courts, a system of public works, means of communication, hospitals, charities, etc., etc.," and that these could only be provided through economic development. As he told President Theodore Roosevelt, "Inasmuch as her geographical position compels us to control and protect her, why not stimulate by moderate assistance those industries which will make her so prosperous and contented that she will be always friendly and a source of strength to us? This certainly is better than having at our doors a demoralized, poverty stricken island, such as Santo Domingo or Hayti [sic] existing under conditions which endanger the lives of millions of our citizens."[10]

Wood articulated a concept of dollar diplomacy that would be increasingly used by the United States after 1900. In this view economic development, sound government, and social order were all tied together. A sound government exercised fiscal prudence and created a situation that would attract foreign (preferably American) capital at reasonable rates of interest. This capital would promote economic development, which in turn would strengthen the government and promote social harmony. Peace, order, and stability would be ensured by the ongoing process of economic development coupled with sound government. Wood and others believed that this would be a mutually beneficial process and that the United States would enjoy increased trade with the developing country.

General Wood and President Roosevelt were convinced that this process was well under way in Cuba by 1902. The insurgents had been persuaded to peacefully give up their arms and most of the leaders accepted the idea that cooperation with the United States would prevent a civil war among the factions. The U.S. Army withdrew from the island, and the new republic formally came into existence on 20 May 1902. The constitution of Cuba contained several articles that the Cuban Constitutional Convention had been required to adopt as the price of American withdrawal. These provisions were known as the Platt Amendment, as Senator Orville Platt of Connecticut (in coauthorship with Secretary Root) had added them to the U.S. Army appropriations act of 1901. The articles placed certain limitations on the actions of the Cuban government in the areas of contracting public debt, making military arrangements with foreign powers, and repudiating acts of the military government. In addition, the amendment gave the United States the right to intervene in Cuba under certain circumstances and stipulated that Cuba would sell or lease "lands necessary for coaling or naval stations." Secretary Root promised a Cuban delegation that the United States would only intervene under the most extreme conditions of anarchy and pledged the Roosevelt administration's support for special treatment for Cuban sugar in the American market. The latter promise was implemented in 1903, after a hard battle with domestic protectionists.

The Platt Amendment was the product of many minds and a compromise between those who wanted to exercise a decidedly imperial role in the Caribbean and those who wanted a rather general kind of predominent U.S. influence. Root considered the 1903 treaty with Cuba embodying the Platt Amendment as the incorporation of the Monroe Doctrine into international law. In historical terms, it was the interpretation of the Monroe Doctrine that had been gradually emerging since the 1880s. It certainly embodied the widespread belief that, in the words of General Wood, "there is no escaping the fact that, even if we do not own the island, we are responsible for its conduct, the maintenance of a stable government, and the just and equitable treatment of foreigners residing thereunder."[11] The basic ideas involved helped to shape the Caribbean policies of the United States for the next three decades.

The United States was not the only nation taking an increased interest in the Caribbean. In 1903 the Imperial German Admiralty prepared Operations Plan III, a contingency plan for war against the United States, fought in the Caribbean arena. This plan envisaged the occupation of Puerto Rico by an army of some 15,000 men and the use of bases on the island to conduct a naval offensive against the United States. In 1906 the plan was scrapped as German plans and attentions were directed more to Europe and the shifting alliance structure.

German ambitions in the hemisphere remained much as they had been in 1900 when the German ambassador to Mexico noted in a dispatch that a German colony in Latin America would be of more value than all of Africa. Kaiser Wilhelm II wrote in the margin, "Correct, that is why we must be the 'paramount' power there." This German-American rivalry was an important factor underlying the expanded role of the United States in the Caribbean–Central American region. The German admiralty did not hide its desire for bases in the Caribbean to control an isthmian canal, and to U.S. leaders it seemed that the German-American naval confrontations in the

Samoan Islands (1888) and Manila Bay (1898) might be repeated much closer to home.[12]

Kaiser Wilhelm II once declared that he wanted a place in the Caribbean "where we can drive in a nail and hang our armor on it." Rumors of a possible war with Germany circulated periodically in the United States during the early years of the century. In 1913 the U.S. Navy General Board formulated the Black War Plan, a defensive operation based on a German attack against the Western Hemisphere. The board stressed that when strong enough, "Germany will insist upon the occupation of Western Hemisphere territory under the German flag, and the United States will then have to defend her policy by force, or acquiesce in the occupation." It should be noted that Germany consistently refused to recognize the Monroe Doctrine, and Germany's Admiral von Tirpitz and other naval officers referred to it as that "insolent dogma."[13]

The Venezuelan crisis of 1902–3 provided a new stimulus to the German-American rivalry and convinced Theodore Roosevelt that the United States had to extend its power beyond Cuba and Puerto Rico. Prior to this Roosevelt had stated that Latin American nations could not abuse foreign interests and expect to hide behind the Monroe Doctrine. In cases of misbehavior by such a country, "let the European country spank it."[14] The president seemed to acquiesce at first in the British-German-Italian pacific blockade of Venezuela, instituted on 9 December 1902. Several Venezuelan ships were sunk or captured, and some coastal forts were shelled by the combined squadrons. The Venezuelan dictator, Cipriano Castro, accepted the international arbitration he had earlier rejected, but the blockade was turned into an official wartime blockade pending a final settlement. Then on 17 January 1903 a German gunboat leveled Fort San Carlos guarding the Straits of Maracaibo. Other incidents followed, and Roosevelt informed the German ambassador that Admiral George Dewey had secret orders to be prepared to sail for Venzuelan waters on an hour's notice. Dewey had a fleet of 54 ships based at Culebra Island, Puerto Rico. On 13 February the British and German governments signed a protocol lifting the blockade.

From 1901 to 1903 Roosevelt engaged in a variety of actions to strengthen the American position in the Caribbean. Besides assembling a fleet at the island of Culebra, the president transferred the island to the Navy Department, attempted to purchase the Danish West Indies from Denmark, dispatched a secret expedition to scout the Venezuelan coast for possible landing sites, and sent a naval envoy to help Venezuela prepare for an invasion. This burst of activity and veiled show of force was related to the Caribbean frontage of Venezuela and to the fact that U.S. efforts to acquire an isthmian canal site were in the final stages.

With the securing of the Panama Canal Zone in 1903, construction of the waterway to join the Atlantic and Pacific oceans began and the United States acquired a stake in the Caribbean/Central American area that strengthened the belief that the country must exercise more control there. In December 1902 the British prime minister, Arthur Balfour, quietly slipped the word to Roosevelt that his government would be more than happy to see the United

States police the "troublemakers" in Latin America and said that Britain was prepared to remove its naval forces from the Caribbean. In 1904, when the Dominican Republic went bankrupt, Roosevelt accepted the invitation and asserted a doctrine of preventive intervention, called the "Roosevelt Corollary" to the Monroe Doctrine. He labeled such interventions as "the exercise of an international police power."

Thus Roosevelt extended the basic premise behind Cuban pacification and the Platt Amendment to the Caribbean–Central American region and clearly enunciated an American sphere-of-interest. In the case of the Dominican Republic, Roosevelt signed a pact giving control of customs collecting to U.S. authorities; who in turn would handle the country's revenues so as to provide a portion to settle the debt that U.S. officials had scaled down. Because the Senate did not approve the original pact, Roosevelt had to proceed under an executive agreement until a modified treaty was approved in 1907.

With the advice of the conservative Elihu Root and faced with domestic opposition and the frustrations of a "civilizing mission," Roosevelt came to accept limitations on the tactics used to enforce the American sphere of interest. He most reluctantly sent troops to Cuba in 1906 when Cuban politicians brought the government to a halt and anarchy threatened. The second intervention, from 1906 to 1909, was another attempt at republic building in the Caribbean, and Roosevelt had begun to feel that the United States suffered from distinct limitations in such endeavors. He confided to the editor-diplomat Whitelaw Reed in 1905 that he could see many difficulties in "the control of thickly peopled tropical regions by self-governing northern democracies."[15]

In 1913 Thomas Woodrow Wilson became president of the United States—his administration was deeply rooted in the secularized, Calvinistic vision of the redeemer nation with a peculiar mission and destiny. One twentieth-century manifestation of this tradition was the Progressive movement, with its urge to reform the world. Wilson's secretary of the interior, Franklin K. Lane, succinctly expressed this mood and its connection to a belief in cultural superiority: "There is a great deal of the special policeman, of the sanitary engineer, of the social worker, and of the welfare dictator about the American people. . . . It is one of the most fundamental instincts that have made white men give to the world its history for the last thousand years."[16] To Lane and other believers in the new Manifest Destiny, Rudyard Kipling's "White Man's Burden" was the noble task of nation building and peace-keeping.

Under the guidance of the stern professor Wilson, the United States became more militarily involved in the Caribbean–Central American region than it had been at any time in its history. In part this was a reflection of the war in Europe that not only exacerbated the fear of Germany but also posed the opportunity to reduce overall European influence. In 1915 the new secretary of state, Robert Lansing, wrote (with Wilson's approval) that the "national safety" of the United States depended on intervention to suppress

U.S. Marines in Santo Domingo, Dominican Republic, 1916. Source: National Archives.

insurrections and aid the people in "establishing and maintaining responsible and honest governments." Disorders broke out in Haiti and the Dominican Republic, and the French and the Germans hinted at possible landings. Wilson ordered Marines and Navy Bluejackets to go into Haiti in 1915 and the Dominican Republic in 1916. These were not temporary landings. Both countries were placed under militrary governments and then provided with a constitution written by Americans. In each case the ratification of the document was facilitated by the Marine Corps. In 1916 a special act was passed by Congress authorizing the detailing of U.S. military personnel to serve in the National Guard of Haiti with full Haitian rank. Another such act provided the same for the Dominican Republic. The U.S. ambassador to Great Britain, Walter Hines Paige, described this policy to amused British officials as "shooting" people into self-government.[17]

A variety of sanitation, public health, education, and communication projects were undertaken in both countries as the reforming zeal of the neo-Puritans was once more turned to nation building. In Haiti, however, the armed resistance from the mulattoes resulted in the deaths of approximately 3,250 Haitians. Yet everything that took place during the attempts to create constitutional republics was not necessarily planned or approved by officials in Washington. To a Marine in the Haitian bush, nation building looked quite different from the way it looked to an academic in the White House.

In 1916 the United States purchased the Danish West Indies and thereby occupied a vantage point controlling every major passage into the Caribbean. And in 1917 a U.S. Marine force was sent to Cuba to protect sugar properties and mining facilities. By 1919 the Navy Department, responding to a State

Department inquiry about the possible use of Marines in another situation, said that it had run out of Marines.

The Republican leadership of the 1920s did try to restrict military activity in the area, even though it did not repudiate such action. Marines were removed from Cuba in 1922, the Dominican Republic in 1924, and Nicaragua in 1925 (only to return in 1927). The Haitian occupation continued, but plans for withdrawal had been made by 1933. The use of temporary landing parties was also placed under restraints that had not existed previously. Moreover, during the numerous revolts that took place between 1929 and 1933, the State Department refused all requests for armed intervention. President Herbert Hoover stated frankly that he did not want the United States represented abroad by Marines.

The Marines returned to Nicaragua in 1927 to uphold the Central American Treaty of Peace and Amity, which was designed to discourage the overthrow of elected governments. When the faction led by Augusto César Sandino refused to accept the mediation actions of the United States and began a guerrilla war, the Marines became bogged down in an effort to defeat his forces. Some Marine officers wanted to destroy Sandino's force, but the administration decided that U.S. forces were not to become involved in Nicaraguan politics. The idea was to construct a legal compromise as quickly as possible, provide a politically neutral national guard to sustain the treaty provisions, and then to remove the U.S. presence. Things did not work out exactly as planned, but the last of the Marines departed from Nicaragua on 2 January 1933.

Franklin D. Roosevelt became president in 1933 and announced the "Good Neighbor Policy" for Latin America. This policy did not begin with a master plan—and such an overall strategy was never developed—but like much of the New Deal it grew and grew. The policy began to furnish much of its own momentum as the rhetoric and imagery of Good Neighborism created an atmosphere that made some policy decisions easier than others. The policy also was influenced by developments in Latin America, especially the surge of economic nationalism, and after 1936, by events in Europe and Asia.

In many respects the policy was characterized by ambiguity and confusion. In part this was produced by conflict within the State Department, between State and other departments (especially Treasury and War), and between the administration and powerful congressional factions. Some of the issues involved were the support of (or opposition to) dictatorial regimes, the supplying of arms to various governments, the use of government influence to protect American property, and U.S. trade policy. These conflicts over the meaning and application of the policy resulted in a variety of paradoxical programs and attitudes. Some paternalistic meddling was involved, as were programs for a system of reciprocal relations based on the ideal of equality of treatment.

In general terms Roosevelt, Secretary of State Cordell Hull, Sumner Welles of the State Department, and other policy makers wanted to maintain (and strengthen) the U.S. sphere of interest in the Caribbean–Central American region and to extend the nation's influence in South America. For the most part, they hoped to accomplish these objectives through cooperative, peaceful means. After some confusing twists and turns in 1933–34, most wanted to encourage economic liberalism in the hemisphere to promote the prosperity of all nations and the development of more friendly relations. During the latter half of the 1930s many officials also became concerned over the possibility of German efforts to create client states in the hemisphere through both direct military intervention and indirect subversion by Nazi elements. None of the general definitions of interests dictated any specific policy, however, and as a result the ambiguous evolution of the Good Neighbor Policy was anything but an exercise in monolithic planning and decision making. Bureaucratic power politics became a part of the situation as a host of new government agencies were created to implement the policy. These new agencies (and the expanded, older ones) often competed, and sometimes overlapped, in their responsibilities. One could almost argue that by 1940 the definition of Good Neighbor depended on which department or agency happened to be speaking.

Roosevelt's pre-1933 discussion of issues with his advisors did not produce any specific plans for implementing the general ideas. Thus in 1933, when the Roosevelt administration faced its first Caribbean crisis in Cuba, the field was wide open for experimentation. A variety of policies and actions were suggested and implemented with a considerable degree of confusion. Cuba served as a kind of laboratory for Caribbean policy, and as a result some of the experiments became part of the administration's Latin American policy while others were dropped. Roosevelt and Hull avoided armed intervention, and the Good Neighbor Policy was launched into rough and uncharted seas.

U.S. relations with Cuba provide a good example of the paradoxes and problems involved in trying to implement a Good Neighbor Policy in a country intricately tied to the United States and regarded as vital to the security of the Caribbean. Roosevelt came into office determined to end political unrest on the island. Sumner Welles went to Cuba to pressure President Gerardo Machado y Morales into reaching an accommodation with the orthodox political opposition. Roosevelt and his advisors believed that such a political compromise, when combined with economic measures (i.e., a trade agreement providing for larger imports of Cuban sugar by the United States), would lead to Cuba's economic well being, order, and stability. In turn, this would increase markets for U.S. goods. Ambassador Welles thought that these tactics were working until a general strike swept the island in August 1933. He decided that Machado would have to be removed, and he began working on a plan with the leaders of the opposition. Ranking army officers ousted Machado on the night of 11 August and adopted the Welles plan.

This solution collapsed on 5 September, when the noncommissioned officers of the Cuban army, led by Sergeant Fulgencio Batista y Zaldívar, took control of the army. The leaders of the "Sergeants' Revolt," in conjunction with various revolutionary groups (the most important being the student-faculty groups from Havana University), then took over the government.

Welles surveyed the wreckage of his diplomatic efforts and promptly branded the new government as "ultraradical" with "frankly communistic" theories. In fact, the new government was composed of nationalists holding a variety of reformist and radical views; the Communist party of Cuba would not support it. Military intervention was to be prepared for but held as a last resort. After all, the use of force would have a serious effect on the image of the Good Neighbor. Welles, Roosevelt, and Hull worked out a three-pronged approach: (1) nonrecognition, (2) reliance on the economic exigency created by the depression to make any regime more subject to diplomatic pressure, and (3) working for a deal with Batista, the new military leader. The official line was that recognition would be granted when the government of Ramón Grau San Martín proved that it was able to maintain law and order. He was unable to do this.

After four months of "watchful waiting" Batista decided to accept the benefits Welles had strongly hinted would be available to a cooperative regime. In January 1934 he ousted Grau San Martín and, after a three-day interim presidency, installed the old-line politician Carlos Mendieta as president. The United States recognized the new government within a week.

The Roosevelt administration moved rapidly to help stimulate the Cuban economy and provide prestige for a new government. The Reciprocal Trade Agreement of 1934 lowered the U.S. duty on Cuban raw sugar and gave U.S. goods various concessions in the Cuban market. The Jones-Costigan Act created a "closed sugar area" with a government-run marketing quota system for all sugar consumed in the United States. Cuban sugar received a quota of 28 percent of the market for 1934. The Second Export-Import Bank made two silver loans to serve a double purpose: the stimulation of the U.S. economy and the stabilization of the Cuban economy. The new regime also received a public relations assist when the United States negotiated a new treaty abrogating all of the Platt Amendment except for the Guantanamo Bay lease.

In many respects Batista was a symbol of the paradoxical nature of the Good Neighbor Policy. As if to illustrate this point, the War Department invited him to attend the Armistice Day ceremonies in Washington, D.C., in 1938. Batista and Roosevelt attended ceremonies at Arlington National Cemetery together, and the colonel went on to New York State to review the cadets at West Point. Within the State Department, however, there was growing dissatisfaction with the Batista dictatorship and concern over the dilemma of a nation with democratic ideals supporting an authoritarian regime. FDR's pragmatic approach was, "He may be an S.O.B. but he's our S.O.B."[18] In 1944 Batista heeded the warning signs from Washington and authorized free elections. As a result Grau San Martín returned to the presidency.

The Roosevelt administration faced the dilemma of a depression-bred instability in the Caribbean–Central American region without a clear-cut policy. As leaders with a strong professional military base emerged in several countries, however, U.S. officials accepted them as offering the best chance for stability and friendly relations. Roosevelt clearly did not want to resurrect the Wilsonian policy of trying to remake these governments and societies in the image of the United States. Other options were either nonexistent or unattractive from the viewpoint of sphere-of-influence diplomacy. Thus the Roosevelt administration accepted as the lesser of two evils the regimes of Rafael Trujillo Molina in the Dominican Republic, Anastasio Somoza García in Nicaragua, and Fulgencio Batista in Cuba. Yet there was always a strong element of ambiguity in relations with these leaders, and U.S. officials constantly complained about the difficulty of negotiating with them.

Faced with increasing world tensions after 1935, Roosevelt, Hull, and Welles abandoned the Republicans' Central American Treaty policy (only recognizing governments that come to power by constitutional means) and returned to a policy of recognizing governments that could hold power. This was coupled with a policy of flattery of the leaders and offers of economic assistance. Perhaps Roosevelt, Hull, and Welles went overboard with some of their expressions of goodwill toward these Caribbean strongmen, yet they were also trying to demonstrate a new sense of respect for small nations by according their leaders military reviews, banquets, and glowing speeches. On occasion these relations could take on a comic aspect, as when Ambassador Claude Bowers told Roosevelt about an incident during Batista's visit. The latter left his minister, Martinez, in Washington to handle the sugar agreement while he toured the country. At one party the colonel realized that had had too many martinis. A page came to his table to tell him that he had a phone call from Martinez. "No martinis" Batista replied several times as the page tried to convey his message. The boy's boss sent him back with instructions that he had to make Batista understand. The message was repeated and Batista yelled, "Dammit, dammit, I said I want no more martinis." FDR later wrote to Bowers, "I hope you arranged to see that Batista got plenty of his favorite 'martinis' during his recent visit."[19]

Germany's occupation of France due to its triumphant blitzkrieg campaign in 1940 greatly increased U.S. fears of German actions against the hemisphere, and the sense of anxiety was exacerbated by the fact that the United States had done very little to prepare for its defense. In addition, U.S. officials believed that the country's military weakness and lack of coordinated military arrangements with Latin American nations raised the specter of many of these countries joining the Axis powers in the event that a German foothold were established. Welles told Roosevelt about his concern over the "real danger" of subversive movements and concluded, "I am sure you will agree that if we acquiesce in the creation through the connivance of non-American powers, of governments in some of the American Republics, subservient to Germany, the Monroe Doctrine would be rendered nonexistent and the majority of the American Republics would run helter-skelter to Hitler." In June 1940 Harry Hopkins wrote, "The only assumption it is safe for us to make at this time is that Germany, having won the war within the next few weeks, will proceed immediately in Latin America along the lines clearly indicated by her past and current activities. Her preponderance over us is now at its maximum."[20]

With the German conquest of Western Europe in the spring of 1940 the question of control of the Caribbean colonies of France and the Netherlands became a critical issue to the United States. In June the State Department strongly reiterated the no-transfer of territories doctrine. This became one of the main issues of the Havana Conference of July 1940, and the result was the Act of Havana concerning the Provisional Administration of European Colonies or Possessions in the Americas. This act provided for the provisional administration by an emergency committee composed of one representative from each of the American republics in cases where such colonies were in danger of changing hands. The formal treaty established an Inter-American Commission for Territorial Administration.

In September of 1940 the United States acquired a chain of Caribbean bases in British territories as a result of the destroyers-for-bases deal. In return for the transfer of 50 overaged destroyers the United States obtained 99-year leases for bases in Bermuda, the Bahamas, Antigua, St. Lucia, Trinidad, and Jamaica. Later the Netherlands granted base rights on the islands of Curacao and Aruba. U.S. naval patrols, which had been operating in the Caribbean since 1939, were increased, especially around the island of Martinique to warn the French not to allow the Germans to use the French colonies as bases. In September 1941 Roosevelt received permission from Queen Wilhelmina of the Netherlands to move troops into Surinam (Dutch Guiana) to protect the bauxite mines that produced 60 percent of the ore required by the American aluminum industry.[21]

After the Japanese attacked Pearl Harbor on 7 December 1941, all nine of the Caribbean states quickly declared war. Cuba and the United States signed an agreement in June 1941 granting the latter a base on the western tip of Cuba for antisubmarine patrols. The Dominican Republic and Haiti also gave the United States the right to establish naval bases. In February 1942 a German U-boat attacked Aruba and sank 5 tankers and damaged another; the craft surfaced and then fired on an oil refinery. In March German U-boats sank 21 U.S. ships, and in May 35 went to the bottom. By the end of the year some 336 Allied ships had been sunk. Subsequently, antisubmarine patrols reduced the losses to 35 in 1943 and to three in 1944.[22]

During World War II the United States had an extremely significant impact on the Caribbean region. Islands that had not been touched by the economic, political, or cultural presence of the United States were suddenly inundated by a Yankee tide of men, money, and cultural values. One author called it a large dose of "American breeziness, color discrimination, unconventionality, big money, big ideas, goodwill, and ignorance of the rudiments. of colonial policy."[23]

The U.S. economic impact on the Caribbean was tremendous. In 1942 the United States agreed to buy all the cotton Haiti could produce until the end of the war, and similar agreements concerning sugar were signed with Cuba, Haiti, and the Dominican Republic. The spending that resulted from the building and manning of military bases also had a major impact. Suddenly, jobs were available at more than twice the old wage. Jobs of all kinds were created both on and off military facilities. An American pop song of the period—"Drinking Rum and Coca-Cola"—describes the experience. To a Latin beat the song tells of the Yankees coming to the island; "the native girls all going wild," and both "mutha and daughter working for the Yankee dollar"—the type of work that requires one on the next day "to sit in hot sun and cool off."

The Yankee impact produced tensions and agitation, as well as prosperity. The new wage scale created problems between the Americans and the old colonial authorities—the latter fearing that the higher wages being paid to the islanders would destroy the existing socioeconomic order. Americans criticized colonialism and talked about autonomy and voting. As a result, pressures grew in various colonies for reform. The anticolonial rhetoric of Americans, however, was contradicted by the Americans' racial discrimination. These attitudes produced a conflicted view of the United States among the peoples of the Caribbean. A story came out of one British colony to the effect that an islander was asked to compare the differences in working for the British and the Americans. The man replied that the British give you 50 cents an hour and call you Mister, the Americans gave you $1.50 and call you "Hey George."[24]

To cope with the many problems developing and to plan for the postwar era, the United States pushed the creation of the Anglo-American Caribbean Commission in 1942. The British joined in the hope that the commission could handle emerging problems and expectations (France and the Netherlands joined later in the war). The commission took the lead in developing a coordinated, integrated approach to the region's problems, stressing that the problems must be dealt with on a regional, rather than a local, basis, and that economic diversification was needed. U.S.-British cooperation addressed such areas as health, education, social welfare, labor problems, and agriculture.

President Roosevelt and the commission's head, Charles W. Taussig, believed that the body also had a long-range function of influencing colonialism throughout the world by setting an example of enlightened policies in the Caribbean. As Taussig wrote to FDR, "It seems to me the time is at hand when by using our possessions in the Caribbean as the spring board you could pave the way for a 'charter' granting more political freedom to all Colonial people." He further noted that "the Caribbean perhaps is the only area in the world where it is possible during the war to give a preview of what the post war world may look like." Some British officials were uneasy with the growing U.S. influence on the British colonies, but most—even Churchill, the defender of the empire—realized that the Caribbean was in the U.S. sphere of defense and that Anglo-American cooperation was vital.[25]

With the death of FDR in April 1945 the main driving force behind the commission was gone. It would last into the postwar era but with little influence or direction.

When World War II ended in 1945 American servicemen wanted to get home and return to a normal, civilian life. Programs, plans, and grand designs for the Caribbean became a low priority for the United States immediately after the war ended. The great crusade was over—in more ways than one.

During the war the Caribbean's strategic and economic importance to the United States reached a new high: the United States assumed almost full responsibility for defense of the region and bought almost all of its export goods produced. The United States and the Caribbean were bound together as never before. The end of the war brought a sudden reversal for the United States, however: in every respect the area declined rapidly on the scale of U.S. priorities. Like a rejected lover, the Caribbean countries reacted with a mixture of anger and pretended disdain.[26]

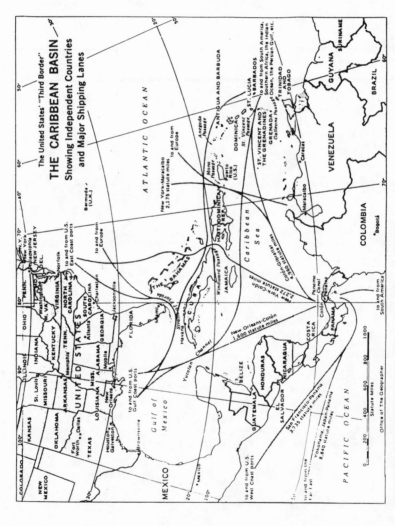

The United States' "Third Border"

THE CARIBBEAN BASIN

Showing Independent Countries and Major Shipping Lanes

From the Bureau of Public Affairs, Department of State, May 1982.

chapter 2

THE POSTWAR WORLD AND THE CHANGING
NATURE OF RELATIONS, 1945–1952

With the end of the war, many Latin American leaders expected a cornucopia of goodies to open up in the United States. Visions of economic development, vastly improved standards of living, and general well-being filled the heads of many. In the Caribbean these visions were further enhanced by the development of an almost xenophobic nationalism. Rising tensions and conflict developed on several islands. For the United States, however, the Caribbean was only one small element in a basketful of worldwide problems, and with the security threat eliminated the area fell low on the scale of foreign-policy priorities. To understand U.S. policy—or lack thereof—and actions in the Caribbean, it is necessary to understand the overall context of U.S.–Latin American policy and problems after the war.

The word that best describes the making of Latin American policy in the immediate postwar period is confusion. During the war agencies proliferated in all branches of government, producing personal rivalries, conflict over jurisdiction, and immense complexities in both the development and implementation of policy. In addition, the State Department was reorganized several times between 1944 and 1948, which produced even more confusion. Latin America was most susceptible to policy-making problems because it was so dependent on personal representation at the highest levels of government. Without such, Latin America tended to be ignored, and diplomats from the area often had to deal with low-ranking U.S. bureaucrats. This caused considerable resentment in Latin American diplomatic circles. Nelson Rockefeller recalled a conversation with Lleras Camargo of Colombia about the unhappy state of relations between the Latin American nations and the

United States during the later 1940s. Rockefeller asked him why he did not go over to the State Department and take up some of the troublesome questions. Camargo replied, "Well, frankly, who would I talk to? The people who do understand and who are handling these problems have no position in the Department. Therefore, if I go over and talk to them and put the heat on them, about these questions, it would just embarrass them, they will be sore, they will react, and it will be to our further disadvantage."[1]

Until his forced resignation (for homosexual conduct) in 1944, Sumner Welles had served as the Roosevelt administration's Latin American policy expert. This role was based on his personal ties with President Roosevelt, and it gave Latin American officials direct access to the highest circles of the U.S. government. With Welles gone, policy making and implementation for Latin America fragmented as the region was relegated to the back burner of American foreign policy. As late as February 1948, George F. Kennan, head of the State Department's Policy Planning Staff, confessed that a document on U.S. foreign policy had no chapter on Latin America, "because I am not familiar with the problems of the area, and the staff has not yet studied them."[2]

The shakeup in personnel dealing with Latin America began with Welles's resignation and Secretary of State Cordell Hull's purge of all officials who disagreed with his Argentina policy. (Under a military dictatorship, Argentina had belatedly broken relations with Japan and Germany in January 1944 but continued to pursue a pro-Axis policy. Secretary Hull advocated diplomatic and economic pressure to force the Argentine government to be more cooperative. Welles and others opposed this policy as a form of intervention.) In a detailed study of Hull's vendetta against Welles, Irwin R. Gellman noted that when Welles was forced to resign in September 1943, "the work of a decade went with him. No one remained to carry out his programs, for Hull and his followers monitored Welles' associates to purge them for suspected disloyalty." Lawrence Duggan, who had helped to shape the Good Neighbor Policy, was one of the victims. When Hull resigned in late 1944, Edward Stettinius became secretary of state and, despite objections, was forced by the president to make Nelson Rockefeller the assistant secretary of state for Latin America. Rockefeller had direct access to the president on matters of Latin American policy. As he noted, "With it you are safe, and without it you have no position of strength if someone with access to the President wants to oppose you."[3]

In June 1945 Stettinius was removed, and James Byrnes became secretary of state. Rockefeller noted that under the new regime, "there were no staff meetings called, nobody saw the Secretary although we were all available."[4] Rockefeller was promptly removed, and Spruille Braden moved into the office of assistant secretary of state for Latin American affairs—the third in less than a year.

The lack of direction in Latin American policy making was noted by the U.S. Ambassador to Brazil, Adolf A. Berle, Jr., in September 1945. He wrote, "We had to make our own line of policy as best we could, nobody being there to give us any guidance." He believed that Braden would do the best he could but that Secretary Byrnes was not interested in Latin America. In addition, the "top group" in the department, he argued, were "solidly European in their interests," and that others took Latin America for granted.[5]

In January 1947 Byrnes resigned, and General George C. Marshall became secretary of state. In June 1947 Spruille Braden resigned, and Norman Armour was brought in to fill a new position—assistant secretary of state for political affairs. As such, he was in charge of all the geographical offices, and the special slot of assistant secretary of state for Latin America affairs was eliminated.

An important facet of U.S. policy making was the running battle between the practitioners of two general approaches to Latin America. The names of the characters might change, and some would even change positions, but the basic conflict would remain to complicate the policy-making process. Over the years, in effect, U.S. policy would tend to swing like a pendulum between two poles. On the one side the "reformers" believed that U.S. policy should actively promote in Latin America a varied program of democracy, social reform, and human rights. The advocates of this approach would vary in their methods in trying to influence Latin American nations to adopt certain policies. Various forms of economic and political pressure—combined with considerable preaching—would be the most popular. On the other side the "realists" argued that the United States could do little, if anything, to change the political, economic, or social conditions in Latin America and should basically follow a policy of supporting those who were friendly toward the United States. To proponents of this position the United States should be more interested in basic security questions than in moral or political perfection.

The reformers' control of the State Department in 1945–46 was in part a reflection of the wartime crusade against fascism and dictatorships. Career Diplomat Ellis O. Briggs argued that "although on short range our policy of standing by democratic principles may crack the *Paper Mache* facade of unanimity it will nevertheless on long range serve to identify us with forces in all of the other American republics which stand for those things for which we declared we were fighting the war. The 'unanimity' behind which the Peróns, Somozas, Trujillos, etc., can take indefinite shelter is neither the one which we should support nor the one wherein any real unanimity among the peoples of the world—as distinct from their governments—can long endure."[6] In November 1944 the State Department sent to all embassies in Latin America an explanation of the nation's policy toward authoritarian governments in the hemisphere. In large part this was provoked by accusations that lend-lease aid was supporting dictatorships and enabling them to remain in power by force. The Brazilian Ambassador, Adolf A. Berle, Jr., explained that the United States did not have the right to intervene in order to unseat dictatorships but that it felt a "greater affinity and warmer friendship for those governments which rest upon the periodically and freely expressed consent of the governed."[7]

The State Department also started a policy of publicly advising American businessmen not to give money to Latin American politicians, bribe officials, or interfere in any way in the internal politics of Latin American countries. Spruille Braden was instrumental in devising this policy while he was ambassador to Cuba from 1943 to mid-1945. He obtained President Roosevelt's approval for this policy and credited it with the election of Ramón Grau San Martín in 1944. Braden believed that this policy had created such confidence among Cuban voters in the integrity of the election that they had rushed to the polls to defeat Fulgencio Batista's candidate.[8]

In like manner, when Colonel Irving A. Lindberg, collector general of the customs of Nicaragua, cooperated with President Anastasio Somoza in putting down a general strike the department instructed the American ambassador to reprimand him. The department's main concern was that Lindberg's action would give the impression that the United States wanted to maintain a dictator in office.[9]

In addition to Argentina the State Department also became very critical of the regimes of Rafael Trujillo in the Dominican Republic and Somoza in Nicaragua. By 1944 the department was postponing approval of requests by these governments for arms shipments under the lend-lease act.[10]

By mid-1945 the State Department was almost routinely vetoing all requests for military assistance or cooperation by these three countries. On occasion Honduras was included in this group of outcasts. In August 1945 Assistant Secretary of State Braden laid down a rule that under no circumstances should U.S. military officers visit Argentina, and the War Department ordered the Caribbean Defense Command to decline all such invitations. In November 1946 the department overruled the U.S. ambassador to the Dominican Republic, who had recommended that the United States renew the agreement providing for a naval mission. In addition, the State Department pressured other governments (such as Great Britain and Brazil) not to supply arms to the designated countries. In January 1946 the British agreed not to sell arms to Argentina or the Dominican Republic.[11]

In late October 1945 the department took an additional step and urged Somoza to establish freedom of assembly and of the press, to allow the return of political exiles, and to guarantee free elections. The next year Somoza came to the United States for medical treatment and let it be known that he would like to visit President Harry Truman. In contrast to the red-carpet days before the war Secretary of State James Byrnes strongly recommended that "under no circumstances [Somoza] be received at the White House."[12] Perhaps the moralistic tone of the reformers' position was best stated in a memorandum Secretary Byrnes sent to President Truman concerning Trujillo's efforts to circumvent the "disapproval" policy of the United States: "As we are well aware, President Trujillo is the most ruthless, unprincipled, and efficient dictator in this hemisphere. He holds the country in an iron grip, rules by fear, and extracts an annual tribute estimated at $5,000,000 from the economy of the country and the Dominican people. . . . His regime is completely unsavory and we should scrupulously avoid even the appearance of lending him any support."[13]

In a memo of June 1946 William P. Cochran, Jr., chief of the division of Caribbean and Central American Affairs, stated that in upholding a policy of "no aid to the dictators, we are true to the postulates for which we said we were fighting World Wars I and II. We are true to the hopes which so many oppressed peoples of the world have placed in us."[14] As Cochran recommended, Honduras's request for six AT-6 airplanes was quickly rejected.

The reformers also opposed the military staff conversations held by the War Department and various Latin American governments (late 1944 and early 1945) and the proposals by the U.S. military to standardize armaments in the hemisphere. One of the main architects of this position, Spruille Braden, noted that the arms program was undesirable because it would perpetuate the grip of reactionary military groups, promote an arms race, increase the danger of communism by increasing poverty in the countries involved, and "aggravate the destructive effects of future revolutionary upheavals in Latin America."[15]

As a result of such efforts, the reformers helped to scuttle the Inter-American Military Cooperation Act introduced in 1946 and again in 1947. To attract the support of the reformers, the War and Navy departments agreed that they would not support any programs of military training or arms supply to "any country controlled completely by a dictator." As a result of this pledge the State Department reluctantly gave its official support to the acts, but the reformers continued to work behind the scenes to prevent their enactment. In fact, on the Washington cocktail circuit one could hear accusations from military officers that this was further proof of Communist influence in the State Department. This was not an accurate perception, but ironically for a brief time the American left did extol the virtues of such officials as Spruille Braden.[16]

The policy of nonintervention in Latin America was repeatedly reiterated not only in public but also in the private sector of departmental memorandums and policy statements. Undersecretary of State Dean Acheson stated the main elements of what he considered U.S. policy in a 1947 memorandum. He noted that the United States was committed to "exclude domination of any part of this hemisphere by any non-American power either by physical coercion or by infiltration," and that along with this principle went the corollary of "renouncing domination for ourselves." And, "We also renounce economic domination. . . . We are not seeking any exclusive economic position." Acheson further explained that this policy was one of encouraging industrialization to build strong allies, not that of keeping the rest of the hemisphere as raw-material producers only.[17]

Even in the case of a possible revolution in Cuba, Spruille Braden stated in 1945 that "since the only way in which [American investments] could be protected would be through military intervention, they will have to be abandoned and when order is restored then it will be up to us to obtain compensation therefore."[18] In late 1945 the State Department informed all ambassadors that "the Department disapproves of and opposes most strongly any intervention in local political affairs by American businessmen or companies. Such activities are bad for American business, complicate international relations and create serious problems, and are bound to lead to rumors that the department is involved."[19]

In 1947 the crusade against Argentina, Nicaragua, and the Dominican Republic was virtually terminated. For one thing, the idealistic wartime fervor of antifascism was dying rapidly. Also, the great optimism that the newly formed United Nations would promote world peace suffered the same fate. The developing cold war played a role, but it was a limited one in 1947. In November of that year the Central Intelligence Agency issued a report entitled "Soviet Objectives in Latin America," which bluntly stated that Soviet undercover penetration of strategic economic sectors in Latin American countries "is already such as to permit the U.S.S.R. by merely giving the necessary orders to withhold from the U.S. its normal peacetime flow of strategic raw materials from Latin America, and to precipitate economic crises in several Latin American countries." Army and Air Force Intelligence concurred, but Naval Intelligence and the State Department dissented on the grounds that the report gave an erroneous concept of the mechanics and strengths of Soviet influence and exaggerated the "real or latent danger" from communism.[20]

In March 1948 the Policy Planning Staff of the State Department recommended that the United States should not enter into anti-Communist agreements with other American republics and should oppose a multilateral inter-American, anti-Communist Agreement until further study had been given to the situation.[21] This preliminary report became National Security Council Report 16 (28 June 1948) on "U.S. Policy Regarding Anti-Communist Measures Which Could Be Planned and Carried Out within the Inter-American System." Even at this stage of the cold war the report recommended that the United States be very careful in dealing with extreme reactionary "governments that rule through military or dictatorial means."[22]

An important factor leading to the demise of the crusade was that its keystone—the denial of arms and military equipment to dictatorial regimes—was about to crumble. In December 1946 Ambassador to Mexico George Messersmith warned that various nations (including Great Britain, Sweden, Spain, and Czechoslovakia) were "clamoring" to sell such supplies to Argentina. He believed it was time to prevent a "further loss of prestige" and "synthesize a policy somewhere between the extremes represented by the views of Messrs. Hull and Braden, on the one hand, and Messrs. Stettinius and Rockefeller on the other."[23]

At the end of 1945 the United States had suggested that Britain stay out of the Latin American arms market altogether, but the British "politely refused." They did, however, make a gentlemen's agreement with the United States not to sell arms to Argentina or the Dominican Republic.[24] By late 1946 the British desperately wanted to sell arms to pay for Argentine foodstuffs and to accumulate hard currency. Various British firms saw a lucrative, and available, arms market in Argentina, and Vickers, Thorneycrofts, and Swan Hunter had all approached the Admiralty seeking permission to offer their wares. In January 1947 the British ambassador was instructed to inform the U.S. government "at the moment he considers most appropriate" that the gentlemen's agreement "will terminate in ten days." The "appropriate moment" was judged to be "after the outcome of the Braden-Messersmith battle becomes clear, but regardless of which is the victor."[25] The moment came in late March when the Hawker-Siddely Group asked for approval to sell 100 Meteor jet fighter planes to Argentina. The Board of Trade recommended the sale to the prime minister, and the Foreign Office gave its approval on 3 April.[26]

The British cabinet decided to terminate the gentlemen's agreement on 22 April 1947. Secretary of State Lloyd Perone decided not to speak to U.S. Secretary of State George Marshall personally about the decision. Instead, an aide-memoire was drafted on 30 April and presented to the State Department on 6 May. The Truman administration had already decided to pursue the Messersmith formula, and Marshall confidentially informed Britain's U.S. ambassador, Lord Inverchapel, that the "situation" would probably be cleared up in about three weeks. After that, he noted, the United States would have nothing more to say regarding British arms sales. The "clearing up" Marshall referred to came on 3 June when President Truman announced that the United States was ready to include Argentina in inter-American talks regarding the implementation of the Act of Chapultepec. Two days late Spruille Braden resigned.[27]

Despite some grumbling within the ranks, the State Department moved to eliminate restrictions on arms sales to the blacklisted countries. On 4 August the Dominican Republic's ambassador was informed that his government could now make requests for arms export licenses. On 14 August the British were notified that the United States would not discriminate against any Latin American country concerning arms sales. In the future all would be "measured by the same yardstick." The Canadians were thanked for their "splendid cooperation" on arms matters.[28]

Although the freeze on arms sales to dictators had been eliminated, some of the old emotions and restraints still lingered in Washington. In mid-1949 the Defense Department's draft order of priority of countries for allocation of spaces for training at U.S. service schools had three categories. All Western European nations, Saudi Arabia, Turkey, Brazil, Mexico, and Venezuela were in the top category. Most of the other Latin American nations were in category 2. Argentina, the Dominican Republic, Honduras, and Nicaragua were placed in the last category.[29]

After June 1950 and the outbreak of the Korean War the cold war became much more of an influence in all aspects of U.S. foreign policy. In Latin America the maintenance of friendly regimes became more important than democratic purity. In 1952 General Harry Vaughn, Truman's military aide, wrote a note to the president stating that although Somoza was a "dictator by some standards," he nonetheless was a "firm friend of the U.S.A. and Harry Truman." Vaughn recommended that when Somoza came to the United States "we should give him some recognition plus a dinner and a 'kidney medal.'" Perhaps a little more hesitant than his aide, Truman replied that it would be "rather difficult to take care of him but we will manage it some way."[30] Assistant Secretary of State Edward Miller summed it up best in a note to Thomas E. Whelan, the U.S. ambassador to Nicaragua, discussing the Democratic party convention. He concluded, "You can tell Tacho [Somoza] that whichever of the two wins, he will still have a good friend in the White House."[31]

Postwar nationalism especially affected U.S. relations with Cuba and Puerto Rico. In the case of Cuba, nationalism was mixed with corruption, violence, and an antibusiness policy on the part of the government. Certainly the proximity of the United States and the protectorate role assumed by it after 1898 made plucking the eagle's tail an exciting part of Cuban politics. But the United States had given up the protectorate role and had restored the air base facilities to Cuba earlier than required on the demand of the Cuban government. In addition, American ownership of sugar properties had shrunk from some 60 percent to about 40 percent.

In September 1946 the ambassador to Cuba Henry R. Norweb analyzed the Cuban situation as one in which the Cubans, now convinced that the protectorate had ended, were flaunting their independence in much the same way as "a puppy might yelp bravely at a mastiff behind a fence." But, he noted, "The 'fence' is our own determination that we will not again be lured into 'landing the Marines.'" Norweb summarized the new relationship in these words: "Under the Good Neighbor policy we can do little more than seek to encourage, by every legitimate means, an attitude of responsibility and an atmosphere of stability in which Cuba may make her own way into the community of mature and progressive peoples."[32]

On 10 March 1952 General Fulgencio Batista—the former sergeant who had seized power in the 1930s and stepped down in 1944—led an almost bloodless coup. The United States did not immediately recognize the new government because of the fear "that this kind of thing may occur in other countries of Latin America where elections are being held this year." But after 10 Latin American nations did recognize the Batista government and the general promised to hold free elections, the United States granted recognition on 27 March.[33]

After the war the United States had to face the embarrassing fact that it still held the island of Puerto Rico as a colony. Starting with the Foraker Act of 1900, the United States had begun to liberalize colonial rule. This act provided for a popularly elected House of Delegates, an appointed Council (that also served as an upper house) in which at least five members were to be Puerto Ricans, and an elected president commissioner who would represent the island in Washington. Later this official was given a seat in the U.S. House of Representatives with the right to speak and introduce legislation but not to vote. Puerto Rico was also exempted from U.S. internal revenue laws. In 1916 the Jones Act granted a bill of rights and, an elected upper house and made Puerto Ricans citizens of the United States.

American colonial policy perhaps can best be characterized as "benign neglect." Many of the people of the island were poor, but life expectancy and population were increasing, education was spreading, and the coffee and sugar industries were growing. Then the hurricane of 1929 devastated the coffee industry, and sugar prices fell during the depression of the 1930s. Rexford Guy Tugwell, a New Deal "braintruster" and governor of Puerto Rico from 1941 to 1946 would label the island "the stricken land," the title of his book.

Puerto Rico was torn by violence during the 1930s. The Puerto Rican Nationalist party, led by Pedro Albizu Campos, demanded independence and engaged in several armed clashes with the police. In 1936 members of the party assassinated the island's chief of police, Colonel Francis E. Riggs, and in March 1937 an unauthorized march by the party resulted in what was called the Ponce Massacre. Nineteen people were killed, including two policemen, and more than 100 were injured. Subsequently assassination attempts were directed at a federal judge and Governor Blanton Winship.

After the assassination of his friend Riggs, Maryland Senator Millard Tydings introduced a bill in 1936 to provide the Puerto Ricans a referendum on independence. If approved and a constitution adopted, a four-year transition period would begin. When faced with the termination of economic programs and tariff protection, most Puerto Rican politicians backed away from independence. Only the small groups of radical nationalists supported the Tydings proposal. The U.S. Congress did not accept the bill, but Tydings would reintroduce it several times during the next decade.

President Roosevelt and his wife, Eleanor, were sympathetic to the problems of the island, but both Roosevelt and his confidant Tugwell were perplexed by the island's politicians. The New Deal was extended to Puerto Rico in 1935, and the Emergency Relief Organization and its successor, the Puerto Rican Reconstruction Administration, provided food relief and promoted a variety of programs such as agricultural diversification, public works, and employment. A sum of $57 million was pumped in, but many problems remained. Roosevelt and Tugwell felt that the politicians were largely responsible for the sorry state of affairs. In late 1941 the president wrote to Tugwell, "You ought to put up a sign reading 'the United States helps them that help themselves.' That would give a new thought to the politicos in your midst. You might also tell them, 'Look beyond the end of your own nose.'" He concluded by noting that Tugwell was still young and might make improvements if he could stay 25 years.[34]

Tugwell constantly referred to the "colonial whining" of the politicos and stated his opinion that the nasty nature of Puerto Rican politics was due to the "Spanish-Negro character" of the people—especially the element of "Spanish blood."[35]

Tugwell and Roosevelt understood Puerto Rico better than most academics in that they came to realize the problems for economic and political development crated by the Spanish-Catholic cultural value system. Roosevelt had discussed the problem of birth control and the opposition to it of the Roman Catholic Church with the Archbishop of Puerto Rico, and certainly he knew that in some societies population growth continually outruns economic growth.[36] In 1901 the death rate was 36.7 per 1,000; by 1921 it was 22.3, and in 1941 it had fallen to 18.6. In the process, the population almost doubled.

During World War II prosperity came to Puerto Rico via the spending by both the U.S. government and military personnel, and the excise tax on rum that was returned to the Puerto Rican government. It was not uncommon in mainland liquor stores to require a customer to purchase two or more bottles of rum along with a bottle of American whiskey—if the latter were available.

As a result Americans consumed a lot of rum. Along with prosperity came a new spirit of cooperation between Governor Tugwell and the rising political star, Luis Muñoz Marin. The latter had been expelled from the Liberal party and founded a new one, the Popular Democratic party (PPD), in 1938. He became president of the Puerto Rican Senate in 1940 and, with Tugwell's support, brought a new generation of mostly U.S.-educated young men into public service. Teodoro Moscoso, Enrique de Toro, Jaime Benitez, Rafael Pico, and Roberto Sanchez Vilella were among the new leaders who hoped to reshape the island along noncolonial lines.

Muñoz Marin and Tugwell launched, or attempted to launch, a variety of programs. The Agricultural Corporation bought thousands of acres of land and sold or distributed it to small cane growers, cooperatives, and small farmers. FDR gave his personal endorsement to this action.[37] Among the other 14 public corporations, the Development Corporation was one of the most active in trying to promote Puerto Rican investment in producing glass, paper, cement, and other products. In a controversial move, however, the corporation also tried to drive "absentee" (i.e., U.S.) investment off the island. As a result, some of these measures were opposed by groups in both Puerto Rico and the United States, and some U.S. Congressmen referred to Tugwell as "Red Rex." With the smashing victory of the PPD in the 1944 elections, however, some of this opposition was muted.

In 1943 President Roosevelt called on Congress to change the Jones Act and, among other things, provide for an elected governor. The Puerto Rican legislature in February had passed a resolution asking for greater autonomy. Roosevelt established a Committee for Revision of the Organic Act of Puerto Rico, which produced a bill that the Senate passed in early 1944. The House never took up the measure, as it was completely smothered by very negative reports of conditions in Puerto Rico issued by the House Committee on Insular Affairs headed by C. Jasper Bell. In late 1943 the committee approved a bill that would have eliminated one of the basic elements of the Jones Act. One provision stated that some of the taxes on Puerto Rican products, especially rum, would no longer go to the Puerto Rican government but would be allocated by the U.S. Congress. Secretary of the Interior Harold L. Ickes angrily denounced this proposed legislation and in a letter to Bell declared, "It [the bill] violates every principle of fair dealing and would reduce Puerto Rico to the status of a dependency and a beggar." Ickes further stated that the policy of the United States was one of "progressively increased self-government and control of local affairs," and that passage of the bill would relegate Puerto Rico "to the worst form of colonial domination." Tugwell's protest was milder but did include the idea that the passage of the bill would necessitate statehood for the island.[38] The House committee issued a severe indictment of the Puerto Rican government, which doomed any action on greater autonomy for the time being.

During World War II more than 65,000 Puerto Ricans served in the U.S. armed forces. This included the 295th and 296th Infantry Regiments of the Puerto Rican National Guard. These regiments saw service in the Pacific theater.

Harry S. Truman, who became president when Roosevelt died in April 1945, took an interest in Puerto Rico, and Tugwell gave him an extensive briefing in August. Tugwell wanted to resign, but Truman asked him to remain at his post for a few more months. Charles W. Taussig recommended to the president that he appoint a Puerto Rican as governor and suggested the Resident Commissioner Jesus T. Piñero. The president had been thinking along these lines and informed Tugwell in February of his decision to appoint a Puerto Rican as governor. When Tugwell resigned in June, Truman appointed Piñero as the first native governor.[39] On 4 August 1947 President Truman signed the Crawford-Butler Act that gave Puerto Ricans the right to elect their governor. The United States had begun the process of dismantling the colonial status of the island.

Muñoz Marin was elected governor in 1948 and assumed office in 1949. He immediately began to search for a third path between statehood and independence. He proposed a measure allowing Puerto Rico to create its own constitution to officially establish the self-government being exercised. In July 1950 Congress passed Public Law 600, which eliminated those parts of the Jones Act regulating the internal government of Puerto Rico and provided for a plebiscite on the issue of a constitution and a popular vote on a constitution when drafted. Puerto Rico's relationship with the United States was then defined in the new Federal Relations Act passed on the same day. This act replaced those of 1900 and 1917 but continued the basic elements of common defense, common citizenship, common market, and common currency.

The campaign to approve Public Law 600 began in August 1950 and the violent opposition of the Nationalistic party was led by Pedro Albizu Campos, who had just been released from prison. On 30 October a group of Nationalists assaulted the governor's mansion and others launched uprisings in six towns. When the smoke cleared, 27 people had been killed and 90 wounded. Two days later, two nationalists attacked Blair House in Washington, D.C., in an attempt to kill President Truman. In the ensuing shootout a White House policeman, Leslie Coffelt, and one of the terrorists were killed. Two other policemen and the second terrorist were wounded. The latter's death sentence was commuted by Truman, and President Jimmy Carter would set the terrorist free in 1979. One of the terrorists had a note from Albizu Campos in his pocket, and the nationalists' leader as well as others were jailed.

Public Law 600 was approved by Puerto Rican voters in June 1951 (76.5 percent of those voting); delegates to a constitutional convention were elected; and, in February 1951, the convention finished its work. On 3 March 1952, 80 percent of the voters approved it. The U.S. Congress finally approved the constitution after adding a restriction that any amendments or revisions could not violate Public Law 600, the Federal Relations Act, the terms of the approving resolution itself (Public Law 447), or those portions of the U.S. Constitution applicable to Puerto Rico. Public Law 447 was approved by the constitutional convention, and on 25 July 1952 Governor Muñoz Marin proclaimed the Commonwealth of Puerto Rico. This was also the fifty-fourth anniversary of the landing of U.S. forces.

In approving this document, the U.S. Congress had accepted the words *union* and *compact*. To Puerto Ricans, *union* implied a much stronger relationship than the term *association*, and *compact* meant a mutually binding agreement requiring the consent of both parties before it could be altered. Like the title "commonwealth," these words have not been clearly defined and have different meanings to different people. Just what is a commonwealth? Massachusetts is also called a commonwealth, but its status is clearly different from that of Puerto Rico. Thus even after 1952 the exact political relationship of the United States and Puerto Rico remained ambiguous. As one authority put it, "interpretations of the nature of the relationship vary from that of sovereign co-equals on the one extreme to that of Puerto Rico's being war booty, property, or a colony of the United States on the other extreme. The stage was set for a tug of war that could go on forever."[40]

The Nationalists were not finished with attempts to create trouble and embarrass the United States. On 1 March 1954 four Nationalists led by Lolita Lebron opened fire from the visitor's gallery of the U.S. House of Representatives: five Congressmen were wounded, none fatally. The four, and Albizu Campos, were sentenced to life imprisonment. President Carter pardoned the four in 1979—Albizu Campos had died in 1965, prior to his pardon.

The economic programs of the war years had not broken the cycle of unemployment. As a result the Puerto Rican government backed away from the policy of driving out American capital and instituted policies to attract such capital for industrial development. The Industrial Incentives Act of 1947 provided 10-year exemptions from local taxes, and businesses operating in Puerto Rico were not subject to federal corporate taxes. Thus "Operation Bootstrap" began, and by 1950 the island's per capita income was the highest in Latin America. Between 1947 and 1959 the gross national product doubled.[41]

Clearly, Puerto Rico was no longer a colony in any legitimate sense of the word. Its status was not clearly defined, and legally the U.S. Congress could still impose its will on some issues. But, however defined, Puerto Ricans had a unique status. They enjoyed almost all the benefits of mainland citizens except for representation in Congress. They were exempt from federal taxes and could freely travel to the United States. Puerto Rico in 1952 was vastly different from Puerto Rico in 1940.

At the end of World War II U.S. policy makers hoped to see a peaceful, democratic hemispheric system. Within this system the United States would actively favor democratically elected regimes that promoted the well-being of the people. The days of sphere-of-interest policies seemed to be over. Outside imperial threats to the independence of Western Hemisphere nations seemed to be a thing of the past, and as a result the need for military intervention also seemed to be ended. This scenario would begin to change in the late 1940s, and U.S. policy would follow suit.

chapter 3

THE COLD WAR STRIKES
THE CARIBBEAN, 1953–1969

When Dwight D. Eisenhower became president in 1953 the chill of the cold war had already begun to be felt in the Caribbean area. The main focal point was Guatemala, which had been pursuing an anti-U.S. policy for several years. Not only were American properties seized with little effective compensation, but Guatemala was the only country in the Western Hemisphere to support the North Korean–Soviet position in the United Nations.

In the United States a rising crescendo of angry voices demanded some action by the United States. One of the common arguments stated that if nothing were done about communism in Guatemala, then the loss of American lives in Korea would have been a complete waste. Democratic Congressman Mike Mansfield (Montana) called the situation "dangerous in its implications to the peace and welfare of the Western Hemisphere" and expressed the hope that the State Department and the Organization of American States (OAS) would "take the necessary steps to . . . considered what can be done to bring democracy back to Guatemala and a fair deal to American investors in that country."[1] The *New York Times,* the *Washington Post, Newsweek, Time,* and other publications carried warnings about the Communist takeover in Guatemala. Congressional Republicans had earlier accused Truman of "losing" Guatemala as he had "lost" China. Now the Republican party was in the White House, and the ball was in its court.

The reaction by government officials, Congressman, news media, and others must be set in the context of the fear and sense of isolation produced by the cold war. After the victory of the Chinese Communists in 1949, the two largest countries in the world were ruled by anti-U.S. dictatorships and were allied. According to these countries' own pronouncements, they were dedicated to the destruction of liberal democracy and capitalism around the world. A world map with Communist areas colored red presented a sobering—and even frightening—picture. The Korean War and the massive Chinese intervention in late 1950 further intensified this pessimistic view of world events. Some official studies of the world situation warned that Americans might have to make much greater sacrifices in the years ahead to keep those parts of the world still open from being closed by the new Communist empire.

President Eisenhower was determined not to let Guatemala become the opening wedge of this empire in the Western Hemisphere. In fact, by late 1952 the official policy statement of the State Department declared that the principle of nonintervention in the affairs of Western Hemisphere nations did not apply to regimes that were clearly Communist.[2] The problem lay in deciding when the line had been crossed, and Eisenhower faced that issue in 1953.

Sometime during the summer or fall of 1953, the president instructed the CIA to prepare an operation to oust the government of President Jacobo Arbenz with a bare minimum of direct U.S. involvement. This was not to be a "Marines-over-the-beach" type of operation. Instead, the CIA contacted the exiled opponents of Arbenz and helped them organize a small army. Colonel Carlos Castillo Armas, who had led an abortive coup in 1950, had been receiving some aid from Nicaragua and the Dominican Republic, and the CIA gave its support to his group. The United States provided several old, medium bombers and a clandestine radio station named the Voice of Liberation. There was relatively little fighting during the June 1954 operation, and the radio station thoroughly confused and disrupted the defensive efforts of the Arbenz government. After a large part of the Guatemalan army refused to support Arbenz, the president resigned on 27 June, and a new government, led by Colonel Castillo Armas, came to power. A very limited amount of U.S. assistance had effectively enabled the Guatemalan opposition to overthrow the left-wing regime with relative ease. The United States immediately provided substantial economic assistance to the new regime.

Those officials who knew the details viewed this secret operation as an excellent lesson in achieving foreign-policy victories through very limited, clandestine action. It also reinforced a prevailing view that the governments of most Latin American countries were controlled by a small power elite, and that this was as true for revolutionary governments as for right-wing dictatorships. Thus a small, well-organized Communist group could take over such a nation without too much difficulty, and, conversely, this new form of foreign intervention could be blocked by a new type of limited, clandestine action in support of native, anti-Communist elements. By 1954 U.S. officials did not really consider such action as intervention in the old-fashioned sense, but as necessary defensive measures to counter Soviet, covert intervention.

During the Eisenhower administration the flow of U.S. public and private capital to Latin America doubled, and the shipment of food to needy countries tripled. Plagued by a variety of traditional anxieties, hopes, and dilemmas (all exacerbated by the cold war), the Eisenhower administration adopted substantial elements of the liberal foreign policy tradition, consisting of pro-grams and plans to uplift, reform, and develop Latin America. In its post–World War II stage, this tradition now called for ever-increasing eco-nomic assistance from public coffers. Dwight D. Eisenhower laid the founda-tions and erected much of the framework for the Alliance for Progress of his successor, John F. Kennedy, who would receive most of the credit (or blame) for the new era of U.S. reformist fervor and economic generosity. The Eisen-hower approach was more low key and less emotional.

One can argue that this outburst was fueled by growing fears of Com-munist-directed revolutions that would produce allies for the Soviet Union. Yet this was only part of the story. The old Puritan-inspired ideology of the redeemer nation (at least the activist variant of the tradition) had been a potent element in U.S. foreign policy off and on for over a century and a half. When driven by this ideology, Americans became enthusiastic missionaries of technology, sanitation, education, good government, and economic develop-ment. Uplift, reform, and even regeneration became integral elements in for-eign policy. When combined with a fear of foreign, imperial control of large parts of the world—in effect, closing the open world—an emotional, explosive dynamic was created that could produce a wide variety of contradictory plans, policies, and actions. The evolution of the cold war had gradually pro-duced a renewal of a limited type of U.S. intervention in the internal affairs of hemispheric nations. The ideological renewal, developing in the late 1950s, combined with the phenomenon of a Cuban Revolution following the Marxist-Leninist path to produce more intense and widespread forms of intervention. These would cross the policy spectrum from the landing of 22,000 troops in the Dominican Republic (1965) to the humanitarian activities of the Peace Corps.

The Eisenhower administration bequeathed the problem of Fidel Castro and his Cuban revolution to the Kennedy administration. Castro and his tiny guerrilla group in the Sierra Maestras came along at a propitious moment in the history of U.S.–Latin American relations. Increasing numbers of Ameri-cans (in and out of government) were looking for a "good revolution" to embrace to prove that the United States really did support economic reforms. President Eisenhower was in the process of reshaping his Latin American policy so as to demonstrate concern for reforms. Against this background Castro did an excellent job of portraying himself as a "democratic reformer" and selling this image to the Cuban and American people. Interviews with Castro published in the *New York Times* and *Coronet* magazine, and the televi-sion and radio campaign carried out by his supporters, all pushed the mes-sage of democratic reformism. But Castro was in reality a power-hungry, xenophobic nationalist whose view of the world was much closer to Vladimir Ilyich Lenin than to Adam Smith. In a 1954 letter to one of his devoted follow-ers he wrote, "Deal with the people artfully and with a smile. . . . Defend our viewpoints without making unnecessary enemies. There will be enough time later to crush all the cockroaches together." And in a letter of June 1958 he revealed his true enmity toward the United States when he wrote, "When this war is over a much wider and bigger war will commence for me—the war that I am going to wage against them [the Americans]. I am aware that this is my true destiny."[3] Yet the press releases of Castro's 26th of July Movement declared exactly the opposite view, and even announced that U.S. imperialism was a thing of the past.

The Eisenhower administration had mixed views of the Castro movement between 1956 and 1958. Fulgencio Batista continued to receive American military equipment under the terms of the 1952 Mutual Security Agreement, but pressure grew in Congress and the State Department to drop all support for the Cuban government. In reality, the U.S. government did very little to interfere with the shipment of arms and equipment, or the transfer of funds, from Castro's supporters in the United States to the guerrillas in Cuba. Then, in early 1958, the United States announced an embargo on the sale of arms to the Cuban government. This was the beginning of the end for a corruption-plagued Batista regime. Demoralization of the government affected the army and in effect the regime collapsed—Castro did not win a military victory. In late 1958 some U.S. diplomats tried to put together an interim government to replace Batista until elections could be held. These efforts failed, and Batista fled Cuba on New Year's Eve 1958.

After a brief power struggle with other revolutionary groups, Fidel Castro's 26th of July Movement took control of the country in January 1959 with a government representing various political groups. The United States quickly recognized the new government and a period of cautious relations began. Castro gradually consolidated his power during 1959, first expelling moderates from the government, then all anti-Communists. On Castro's trip to the United States in April (at the invitation of an association of American editors), U.S. officials offered economic assistance to his finance minister, Rufo López Fresquet. But Castro had ordered López Fresquet to decline all offers on the grounds that later it would improve his bargaining position. Shortly thereafter, in a speech in Buenos Aires, Castro called on the United States to donate $30 billion for Latin American economic development. This was completely unrealistic, as it was meant to be.

In 1959 Castro also began to move against foreign businesses, and in May he proclaimed the Agrarian Reform. The U.S. government asked for negotiations on the issue of compensation for U.S. interests, but Castro delayed any meeting with Ambassador Phillip Bonsal until September. Bonsal assured Castro that the United States did not oppose land reform but only wanted fair treatment for Americans who had lost their property. Castro was noncommittal, but by the end of the year the U.S. ambassador was convinced that Castro did not really want to negotiate issues with the United States but instead was seeking ways of deliberately provoking the so-called Colossus of the North.

In a series of moves largely ignored by the United States, the Cuban leader began in April 1959 to reveal his true intentions. On 25 April a group of Cubans sponsored by Castro invaded Panama. This turned into a miserable failure. In the meantime, members of the democratic left and the old Caribbean Legion (a group founded in 1947 and devoted to the overthrow of all dictatorships in the Caribbean) flocked to Cuba in hopes that Castro would

give broad support to their causes. The Nicaraguan veterans of the legion discovered, however, that Castro would not provide them with assistance unless
they accepted the Nicaraguan Communists as full partners (the latter had set
up a Revolutionary Junta in Havana in January) and the Communist Ernesto
"Che" Guevara as director of operations. They refused and launched a futile
attack on their own. The democratic left discovered in the course of 1959 that
Castro was not one of their number.

Castro's most ambitious operation was an attempt to invade the Dominican Republic. This also failed. The Cuban leader began to build a new Cuban
army and spent more than $120 million on arms and equipment before the
end of the year. During the fall Cuban exiles began attacks on the island,
which Castro blamed on the United States in a series of virulent harangues.

In February 1960 a high-ranking Soviet official, Anastas Mikoyan, arrived
in Cuba. A trade agreement was concluded, and later that month the Cubans
signed another agreement with East Germany. On 28 March Castro publicly
repudiated Cuba's obligations under the Rio Pact of 1947. This was a dramatic
gesture to demonstrate Cuba's break with the inter-American system and its
repudiation of friendly relations with the United States.

In June 1960 Castro ordered foreign oil companies in Cuba (Shell, Esso,
and Texaco) to refine a shipment of Soviet crude. This would have required
refinery modifications and, on advice from Treasury Secretary Robert
Anderson, they refused. Castro then nationalized the companies, and President Eisenhower reduced the Cuban sugar quota for the remainder of the
year. Castro launched an all-out war on U.S. businesses. By the end of 1960 all
U.S. and most foreign businesses had been eliminated. Castro confiscated
approximately $1 billion worth of American property with no hint of compen-
sation. Eisenhower then ordered a partial trade embargo (a full embargo
would come in 1962). In January 1961 Castro ordered the U.S. Embassy to
reduce its staff by substantial numbers, and Eisenhower broke relations with
the island.

Meanwhile, however, dramatic developments had taken place in Soviet-
Cuban relations in 1960. In July Soviet Premier Nikita Khrushchev declared
Soviet military support for Cuba and noted that in case of need, Soviet
artillerymen could hit the United States with accurate missile fire. An article
in the Soviet military paper *Red Star* declared that Soviet threats had already
prevented a direct U.S. attack on Cuba. Khrushchev also proclaimed the death
of the Monroe Doctrine and declared "the remains of that doctrine have to be
buried as any dead body is buried so as not to foul the air with putrefaction."[4]
The Soviet leadership in effect declared that it was ready to adopt the Cuban
revolution as part of the new cold war that would be fought in the third
world. Whether countries were independent made no difference; the struggle
would be called "wars of national liberation." Fidel Castro indicated his willingness to accept what he had probably been seeking since mid-1959. He went
to New York in September 1960 to address the U.N. General Assembly, and
his five-hour tirade against the United States repeated every charge the Soviets had ever made and he even added some. Khrushchev gave his new ally a
bear hug and loaned Castro his personal airplane to fly back to Cuba.

Although the craft had ample room, the Cuban left most of his delegation standing in the rain at the New York Airport and blamed the United States for their being stranded.

On 17 March 1960 President Eisenhower authorized the military training of Cuban exiles for a "possible future day." The CIA had initially envisaged the creation of a guerilla force that would operate out of the mountains of Cuba, but plans underwent numerous changes during the year, and the scope of the operation steadily expanded. In June, for example, the decision was made to create a small tactical air force. Eisenhower did not show too much interest in the project, and the incoming president, John F. Kennedy, was presented with a plan that called for the landing of a force of more than 1,000 men at Trinidad. After much debate, Kennedy gave the go-ahead with the reservation that no U.S. forces could be directly involved.

On 1 April the president changed the landing site to Bahia de Cochinos (Bay of Pigs), thus eliminating the possibility of the battalion conducting guerrilla operations, owing to their distance from any mountains. By this time so many changes had been made, and such a variety of operating groups were involved, that the operation had become a mare's nest of complications and contradictions. In addition the CIA operatives in charge of the operation deliberately excluded the anti-Castro guerrillas in the Sierra Escambrays and their representatives in the United States. The administration tried to force the CIA to include Manolo Ray's Movimiento Revolucionario del Pueblo (MRP, or People's Revolutionary Movement), but no effective cooperation was established. The MRP was dedicated to restoring the revolution to its original goals of political democracy and social reform. Ray desperately tried to find out what was going on, but he only received confusing radio signals and no arms. It seems that the CIA operatives did not trust Ray and others because they believed their political views were too far to the left.

The operation began on 15 April when B-26 bombers of the exile air force attacked Cuban airbases in attempts to knock out Castro's small air force. Owing to the international uproar, Kennedy cancelled the planned second attack, and the exile infantry force (Brigade 2506) of 1,453 men landed on 17 April. The plan envisaged the securing of a beachhead to which would be flown the Cuban government-in-exile, led by Dr. José Miro Cardona. This government would declare the formation of a free Cuba and call for international assistance. The Cubans believed that at this point the United States would provide direct military assistance, but Kennedy always insisted that he would not authorize such action.

Castro's air force sank two of the brigade's transports with most of the ammunition and radio equipment. The CIA pleaded with the president to help the brigade, and he did authorize another B-26 attack on Tuesday, 18 April. Clouds covered the beach area, and three of the bombers were shot down. On Tuesday evening the president was called out of a formal White House dinner, and for over two hours CIA officials and members of the Joint Chiefs of Staff argued for U.S. military action. Kennedy refused all actions except one: on Wednesday, 19 April, he permitted navy jets from the USS *Boxer* to fly over the beach for one hour to protect another bomber run, but the latter arrived ahead of schedule. Several B-26s were shot down and the rest driven away. In any case, the navy pilots were not clear as to what role they should play in case of contact with the Cuban air force.

For all practical purposes the ground fighting was finished, and all that remained was for Castro's forces to round up the survivors (who would later be ransomed). Jacqueline Kennedy later wrote that the first time she had seen her husband cry was early on that Wednesday morning when he sat on the edge of the bed and wept. He had publicly promised that there would be no U.S. military intervention, and he held to that pledge even though it doomed the brigade.

At a party in Montevideo, Uruguay, in August 1961 presidential assistant Richard Goodwin found himself face to face with the Cuban finance minister, Che Guevara, who asked Goodwin to thank Kennedy for the Bay of Pigs invasion. Up to that time, he noted, Castro had held a tenuous grip on the Cuban revolution, with the economy in chaos and numerous internal factions plotting against him. The invasion had solidified Castro's power and made him a national hero for having defeated the greatest power in the world. Goodwin replied that Castro could return the favor by attacking the U.S. naval base at Guantanamo Bay (so that Kennedy would have grounds for an all-out attack). Guevara declined the offer.[5]

Nikita Khrushchev believed that his warning to Kennedy that the Soviet Union would assist Cuba had caused the president to back down from an attack on Cuba. This set the stage for the secret Soviet delivery to Cuba of medium-range ballistic missiles and bombers in mid-1962. Kennedy asked the Soviet ambassador about reports of this activity, and the Russian denied everything. U-2 spy planes began to provide photographic evidence of the Soviet's frenzied work on missile emplacements, however, and on 22 October the president delivered an ultimatum to the Soviets: the missiles and bombers had to be removed from Cuba or the United States would take action.

By September the Soviet Union had in place 42 R-12 missiles (1,020 nautical miles range) and planned to send six more. They also were sending 32 R-14 missiles (2,200 nautical miles range), but none had arrived by the time the crisis erupted. The Soviets planned to install at least 40 nuclear warheads. In 1989 a Soviet general stated that 20 warheads had been delivered to Cuba, but at a January 1992 meeting the general's former deputy said that there were actually 36 in Cuba. Still, none of the warhead nosecones had been mated to the missiles—a fact the Cubans were unaware of for some 25 years. At the 1992 meeting the Soviets also revealed that they had installed nine short-range, nuclear-tipped missiles and that authorization had been given Soviet commanders in Cuba to use them in the event of a U.S. invasion. These missiles had a range of 90 miles and were rated at 6 to 12 kilotons. This was the first time that any American was aware of the Soviet readiness to use tactical nuclear weapons in Cuba. Forty-two light Ilyushin IL-28 jet bombers had been unloaded by September, and more were on the way. U.S. intelligence vastly underestimated the number of Soviet troops in Cuba, and Soviets later admitted that some 42,000 combat troops were in place, including at least four motorized rifle regiments. If Kennedy had realized the extent of Soviet combat strength in Cuba he might well have included their removal in the U.S. demands.[6]

The president proclaimed a quarantine of the island and declared that the navy had been ordered to set up a picket line and stop all suspicious Soviet ships in order to prevent the delivery of any more offensive weapons.

Confrontation between the superpowers now seemed inevitable. Soviet ships continued on course to Cuba, work on the missile sites was speeded up, and by the end of the week naval intelligence reported that 50 Soviet submarines were operational in the Caribbean. U.S. military forces were placed on full combat alert, and more than 200,000 troops were prepared to move. This included one Marine and five U.S. Army divisions (two airborne). The navy had 183 ships, including eight aircraft carriers, in the area. On 24 October the Strategic Air Command went to alert status, DEFCON (Defense Command) 2, for the first time in its history. The world seemed to be on the brink of World War III. Some of the president's advisors recommended air strikes to take out the missile sites. Others wanted an airborne invasion. Robert Kennedy, the attorney general, later wrote that after listening to these proposals he passed a note to the president: "I now know how Tojo felt when he was planning Pearl Harbor."[7]

On Sunday, 27 October, Kennedy decided to delay the air strikes against the missile sites for one more day. That same day Khrushchev notified the president that he would pull the missiles out of Cuba if the United States would agree not to attack Cuba. Kennedy accepted orally with the proviso that the Soviets would not in the future place "offensive" weapons in Cuba and that "Cuba itself commits no aggressive acts against any nations of the Western Hemisphere." Kennedy's 14 December letter to Khrushchev did not constitute an iron-clad guarantee on the part of the United States, as the large loophole concerning undefined aggressive acts was included, but his successors would tend to act as if Kennedy had provided a written commitment not to invade Cuba.[8]

Castro was furious over this compromise and sent his troops to seize the missile sites. In all probability he would have attacked Washington, D.C., and New York City had he been successful. But despite casualties the Russians defended the sites, and the crisis of October 1962 ended with what appeared to be an accord. The United States accepted a Soviet ally in its traditional sphere of influence in return for a promise that this ally would not acquire an offensive capability.

The question of the removal of the IL-28 bombers, however, complicated negotiations. Premier Khrushchev flatly refused to pull out the bombers on the grounds that they were only defensive weapons. The Soviets finally agreed to remove the bombers in early December, and the quarantine was finally lifted.

With the failure of the Bay of Pigs invasion, John F. Kennedy demanded an operation to implement his favorite slogan, "Don't get mad, get even." Operation Mongoose quickly became the single largest clandestine operation of the CIA. The Kennedy administration provided over $100 million for it, and Robert Kennedy became the overall coordinator. Some CIA officials had started making plans to assassinate Castro in 1960, and Mafia chiefs who had lost their casinos in Cuba were recruited. During 1961 the number of these plots increased and involved such bizarre elements as poisoned cigars, a poisoned wet suit that would cause a chronic skin disease, and an exploding seashell. The CIA, however, proved extremely inept at what many in the agency regarded as forbidden activity, and in early 1964 the plots were abandoned. Between 1961 and 1963 Operation Mongoose launched a variety of limited, covert actions, but these failed as well. With the assassination of President Kennedy in November 1963, Mongoose died away, as President Lyndon B. Johnson was not, in the words of CIA official Desmond Fitzgerald, "as gung-ho on fighting Castro as Kennedy was."[9] In 1968 the CIA would even warn Castro about an exile assassination plot.

Because of its efforts to foment revolution in Latin America, Cuba was expelled from the OAS in January 1962. These activities declined for a time after Che Guevara's death in Bolivia in 1967, but the Soviet leaders decided that Cuba could play a major role in promoting Soviet-style communism in the third world. As a result the Soviet KGB took over the Cuban secret police (DGI) in 1968, and training camps for terrorists and guerrillas were expanded in Cuba. Castro's earlier, amateur training activities now became more professional, and he would brag (in private) about his role in training the Palestinian Liberation Organization (PLO). The Cuban role in the Soviet military system would become very evident during the 1970s.

Perhaps the most dramatic element in the crusading policy of the early 1960s was the Alliance for Progress. John F. Kennedy assigned the task of expanding the intentions of the Pact of Bogatá, and giving the "new program" a much more ringing declaration of Good Neighbor Policy idealism, to a group drawn from universities, business, and politics. They met at the Harvard Faculty Club in December 1960 and produced the outline document of rather utopian objectives that became the Alliance.

On 13 March 1961 President Kennedy proclaimed the Alliance "a vast cooperative effort, unparalleled in magnitude and nobility of purpose, to satisfy the basic needs of the American people for homes, work, and land, health and schools." He called for a 10-year program of economic development that would eliminate hunger and illiteracy and set all the participants on the road to prosperity. In addition, Kennedy called for social change, especially land and tax reform. "Progress yes; tyranny, no," he declared. His conclusion flung out the banner of crusading idealism emblazoned with the words "Let us once again transform the American continent into a vast crucible of revolutionary ideas and efforts . . . an example to all the world that liberty and progress walk hand-in-hand."[10]

In August the conference of the Inter-American Economic and Social Council met at Punta del Este, Uruguay, to hammer out the details of the Alliance. C. Douglas Dillon, head of the U.S. delegation, informed the assembly that the United States was prepared to allocate more than $1 billion during the first year of the program and some $20 billion in the course of the decade. The greatest part of this would be in the form of public capital provided by

U.S. taxpayers. The Charter of Punta del Este (signed by all except Cuba) called for a minimum economic growth rate of 2.5 percent per year and wide-ranging programs of housing, health care, education, price stabilization, and agrarian and tax reform. Although the document proclaimed programs designed to create and distribute wealth, the emphasis was on government programs rather than on the development of private enterprise.

In a speech to the conference Che Guevara told the delegates that any funds they might receive under the Alliance would "bear the stamp of Cuba."[11] There was some truth to his argument. Certainly the fear that new Communist regimes might come to power as a result of the social and economic problems of Latin America was an important factor in U.S. policy making. But it was much more than fear of Communist regimes that prompted the crusade against poverty: many U.S. officials sincerely believed that the United States could help eradicate misery and poverty, and for a time many believed that the Alliance provided the best mechanism for the job. The Peace Corps was also organized in 1961 and became an integral part of the crusade.

The crusading fervor that blazed in the late 1950s and into the early 1960s touched more than Cuba. The CIA was contacted by groups in the Dominican Republic that were plotting to assassinate Rafael Trujillo and overthrow his regime. The CIA role was very limited, and only a few weapons were supplied. The plotters killed the Dominican strongman in May 1961, and the United States exerted pressure on the new leaders to institute constitutional government and hold elections. When two brothers of the slain dictator threatened to stage a coup in November 1961, units of the U.S. Navy arrived to show the flag. The plot collapsed, and the Trujillo family fled into exile.

In January 1962 the OAS lifted the economic and diplomatic sanctions imposed in 1960 (after a Dominican attempt to assassinate President Betancourt of Venezuela), and the United States immediately reinstated purchases of Dominican sugar and provided a loan of $20 million. After the election of Juan Bosch, the candidate of the democratic left, in December 1962, the Kennedy administration supplied approximately $46 million in Agency for International Development (AID) funds and sent more than 300 Peace Corps volunteers and other specialists to the country.

In September 1963, however, extreme right-wing elements in the military ousted Bosch. Once again the old, and persistent, dilemma of U.S. policy emerged: How far should the United States go in punishing an otherwise friendly country for a retreat from democratic practices? How much chaos would this cause and what would be the consequences? The Kennedy administration, however, was still filled with crusading zeal and initiated stern measures. The United States stopped most economic assistance programs, broke diplomatic relations, and withdrew personnel involved in military and economic assistance programs. The military turned over the government to a civilian triumvirate and promised to hold elections. The United States then recognized the new government in December and restored aid programs.

This uneasy situation prevailed until April 1965, when groups led by the dissident officer Colonel Francisco Caamano Deno ousted the triumvirate and demanded the return of Bosch. The anti-Bosch element among the army officers (the majority) struck back, and what had started as a coup quickly became a civil war. The rebels (or Constitutionalists, as they designated themselves) seized control of most of the capitol and began to distribute arms to sympathetic civilians.

President Lyndon B. Johnson's first reaction was to protect Americans caught in the conflict. Thus on 29 April he ordered Marine forces to go ashore for this purpose. Reports were streaming back to Washington filled with stories of atrocities, violence, and mounting chaos. In addition, intelligence sources informed the president that Dominican Communists were actively involved in the fighting and that Dominicans trained in various Communist countries had been spotted. The president promptly ordered a full-scale military intervention to prevent the victory of the rebels and head off a situation he and other officials believed could present the Communists with an opportunity to assert control over the other groups. Johnson was not about to take a chance on another Cuba. General Bruce Palmer, who commanded the XVIII Airborne Corps in the Dominican Republic, was informed that his "unstated mission" was to prevent another Cuba and at the same time "avoid another situation like that in Vietnam."[12]

The 82nd Airborne Division arrived in the Dominican Republic during the early morning hours of 30 April, and within a few weeks almost 22,000 U.S. troops were on the island. Their first mission was to contain the rebel strongholds; after that there was a great deal of official confusion concerning the right course of action. Johnson clearly did not want to return all the way to the policy of Woodrow Wilson, with the U.S. ruling the island, but he was faced with the dilemma of how to restore order and constitutional government without appointing U.S. proconsuls. Determined to maintain the U.S. sphere of influence, he sent word through his representative McGeorge Bundy to Colonel Caamano Deno: "Tell that son-of-a-bitch that unlike the young man who came before me, I am not afraid to use what's on my hip."[13]

After some initial confusion, U.S. officials devised a policy that would entail a cease-fire, the organization of an OAS police force to enforce it, the removal of the main contenders for power (Caamano Deno on the left, Generals Antonio Imbert Barreras and Elias Wessin y Wessin on the right), and the formation of a compromise government that would restore order and hold elections. One cease-fire was arranged in early May, but it broke down, and the contending forces once more attacked. On 21 May another cease-fire was arranged. Various countries now began to send troops for the OAS police force. Nicaragua, Honduras, El Salvador, Costa Rica, and Brazil (the largest contingent) contributed to the force. In early June Ambassador Ellsworth Bunker arrived to try to work out the compromises that so far had eluded Johnson's special agent McGeorge Bundy. The rebels broke the cease-fire in mid-June, and after two days of fighting the Americans and Brazilians captured 50 blocks of the rebel area and wrecked much of their downtown defense system. Negotiations continued during the renewed conflict.

General Palmer managed to turn the Inter-American Peace Force (IAPF) into an effective agency for peace making. The general finally was able to send the right-wing military leaders out of the country but had some difficulty controlling Brazil's General Hugo Penasco Alvim (named commander of the IAPF), who wanted to crush the Communists and get it over with. Palmer prevailed and reported that he knew the force was a success when signs went up saying "Brazilians Go Home" and "IAPF Go Home" alongside the traditional "Yankee Go Home" slogans. This took a humorous turn when the rebels started selling "Yankee Go Home" T-shirts, and the American troops bought them all as souvenirs. The most popular shirts had the "Yankee Go Home" slogan on the front and "Take Me with You" on the back.[14]

After three months of masterful diplomacy, Bunker, with the able assistance of the CIA (e.g., one agent saved the lives of Caamano Deno and an number of his top aides), negotiated the Act of Dominican Reconciliation and the Institutional Act, which were signed on 31 August 1965 and provided for an interim government that would rule until elections were held in 1966. The military leaders on both sides were givern overseas jobs. Sporadic violence flared until early 1966, but the elections held in June were conducted peacefully. Dr. Joaquin Balaguer won the presidency with 57.2 percent of the vote. He served out his term and won reelection in 1970, thus proving wrong some of the instant (and critical) historians of the Dominican intervention.

In the decade after World War II both economic and political conditions in Haiti seemed to be improving, and U.S.-Haitian relations reached a kind of high point. President Dumarsais Estime paid off the external debt and as a result the last element of U.S. financial control over the Bank of Haiti ended. The office of fiscal representative had been abolished in 1941, but three members of the board of directors of the National Bank were required to be U.S. citizens until the bonds were paid off.

Financial conditions were aided by American public and private agencies, which sent extensive assistance to Haiti. Colonel Paul Magloire (the commander of Garde de Haiti) was elected president in 1950 and continued the push for economic modernization as well as supporting political rights. The U.S. government financed the damming of the Artibonite River to provide both water for irrigation and electrical power. Haiti became the first Latin American country to sign a Mutual Security Agency investment guaranty agreement. This agreement provided U.S. government insurance to protect American investors from expropriation or confiscation. President Magloire, his wife, and his cabinet made a state visit to the United States in January 1955 and were flown from Miami to Washington in President Eisenhower's private plane. The Haitian president addressed a joint session of Congress and declared his unswerving support for the United States in the cold war. Vice President Richard M. Nixon visited Haiti later that year and signed the U.S.-Haitian Treaty of Friendship, Commerce, and Navigation to strengthen economic relations between the two countries.

Devastated by a hurricane in 1955, the Haitian economy fell into an economic crisis. Then, in October 1957, Dr. François Duvalier (better known as

"Papa Doc") became president. For several years after U.S.-Haitian relations were uneasy but normal. Then they entered what can best be described as a long "roller coaster" period. Owing to the increasingly brutal nature of the Duvalier regime, U.S. assistance would be curtailed, then restored, curtailed again, partially restored, and finally canceled. For over two decades U.S. officials were caught in a major dilemma—how to penalize Duvalier without pushing Haiti into chaos and possible Cuban intervention.

In 1959 the United States helped Haiti meet a budget crisis, sent $1 million in surplus food, and provided additional loans for the Artibonite dam project (now over $25 million). The same year Duvalier requested help in modernizing the Haitian military, and the United States sent both a Marine Corps and a navy mission. As if to underscore the urgency of the request, Cuba launched an unsuccessful invasion attempt in August.

Duvalier demanded more economic assistance from the United States, including funds for a jet airport. Officials pointed out that Haiti had received over $40.5 million from 1949 to July 1960, and the loan was not approved. Other forms of economic aid continued as Duvalier played the "give me more or I'll turn to Cuba" card. In January 1962 the United States had to pledge the continuation of aid to secure Haiti's vote for the exclusion of Cuba from the OAS. This was reversed, however, in August when the Kennedy administration suspended most aid in keeping with the pronouncements of the Alliance for Progress. Food for Peace shipments and funds for malaria control were continued.

Two weeks prior to the Cuban Missile Crisis the United States relented and offered to lend Haiti $2.8 million to build the airport near Port-au-Prince. Duvalier would reciprocate by placing the country's harbors and airfields at the disposal of the United States. Early in 1963 Duvalier reversed course. He ordered Marine Colonel Robert Heinl to leave Haiti and launched a purge of the Nacional Garde because he believed it was being forged into an anti-Duvalier force. Almost every member suspected of pro-American sympathies was exiled or killed. The United States also vetoed an Inter-American Development Bank (IADB) loan for a water system in Port-au-Prince and Pétionville.

The Johnson administration began to relax some of the more restrictive aspects of the Kennedy policy and allowed the water-system loan to be made. The Agency for International Development subsequently extended a $4 million investment guarantee for the construction of an oil refinery. The general aid program, however, was not resumed. In 1967 the United States blocked an invasion of Haiti by Cuban and Haitian exiles. The group, led by Rolando Masferrer Rojas, planned to install a Haitian priest as president and then launch an invasion of Cuba.

During the latter 1960s Haiti hovered on the brink of bankruptcy as the Duvalier regime bounced from crisis to crisis. Yet U.S. officials felt much frustration as the only leverage they had was to block Haitian exports to the United States, which would have produced even more misery for ordinary Haitians.

Eisenhower, Kennedy, and Johnson had all grappled with the persistent dilemma of U.S. policy toward the Caribbean—how to promote democracy while protecting American interests. After a trip to the region in 1955, Vice President Nixon reported to the president's cabinet and emphasized "the predominance of one-man rule in these states—the rulers are virtually the governments." Nixon reserved his highest praise for Puerto Rico, which he called the "most democratic of them all," but noted concerning the others that "the United States must deal with these governments as they are and rely on working over a period of time towards more democracy." As for Haiti, the vice president observed that it was "a picture in poverty and pregnancy. He could only hope that they would find some resources to help them along."[15] By the late 1960s none had been found.

chapter 4

THE DECLINE AND RESURGENCE
OF U.S. INFLUENCE, 1969–1992

When Richard M. Nixon became president in 1969 he found U.S. foreign policy in a state of siege. The growing unpopularity of the Vietnam War led a
number of Americans to question U.S. policy in other parts of the world as
well. Some members of Congress began attacking American "imperialism" in
Latin America. These attacks reached a crescendo in the early 1970s, as politicians, academics, clergymen, and others put on figurative hair shirts and
bemoaned the evils of their country. Of course, some Americans have periodically donned the hair shirt of universal guilt and demanded scourging, but
rarely had this posture had such an impact on foreign policy. If an earlier
national mood had held that the world was too evil for the United States, this
one asserted that the United States was too evil for the world.

President Nixon wanted to initiate some new policies toward Latin
America and to give a new emphasis to the "special" aspects of U.S.–Latin
American relations. The president announced the "Good Partner" policy,
along with a program of "action for progress" and the adoption of a "lower
profile" for the United States in Latin America. Nixon's national security advi-
sor, Henry Kissinger, had little expertise or interest in Latin American affairs,
but he did have some apprehension concerning the formation of anti-U.S.
blocs by third world nations. Yet Secretary of State William Rogers and
Kissinger were not expected to be Latin American experts. This was Nixon's
special arena. In addition, he brought back another old Latin American hand,
Nelson Rockefeller, for a special mission to the area. The report submitted by
Rockefeller was promptly sidetracked by a not-too-receptive State Department and by a hostile Congress.

Henry Kissinger became secretary of state in 1974 and generally took a low-key approach to Latin American declarations. In July 1975, at an OAS meeting of foreign ministers in San José, Costa Rica, the United States played a subdued role and quietly supported the revision of the voting rules of the 1947 Inter-American Treaty of Mutual Assistance (the Rio Treaty) to allow the lifting of sanctions against Cuba by a simple majority vote. Kissinger continued to stress interdependence and the willingness of the United States to reach reasonable compromises with developing nations. But the emphasis was placed on concrete economic cooperation, and very little was said about the emotional theme of hemispheric brotherhood and "new" this or "good" that.

Kissinger also continued his low-key policy of gradually establishing relations with Cuba. This had started with the highjacking agreement the two countries signed in 1973. In 1975 U.S. and Cuban officials held secret sessions at U.N. headquarters in New York to explore possible ways to improve relations. The travel radius for Cuban diplomats at the United Nations was extended from 25 to 250 miles, and in August the U.S. government terminated its policy of prohibiting trade relations between foreign subsidiaries of American companies and Cuba. The United States also dropped its policy of black-listing ships engaged in trade with Cuba. In August 1975 these ships were permitted to enter U.S. ports, and the ban on foreign aid to countries trading with Cuba was ended. Yet these overtures were undermined by Cuban military intervention in Africa to support Soviet objectives. In 1975 the Cubans sent a strong military force to Angola to support the Marxist regime, and later troops were dispatched to Ethiopia to assist in that country's war with a former Soviet ally, Somalia. By 1979 the Cubans had approximately 19,000 troops in Angola and between 12,000 and 17,000 in Ethiopia.

In 1969, for the first time since 1898, a battle fleet of a nation hostile to the United States sailed into the Caribbean. During the 1970s the Russians increased the scale of their military buildup in Cuba and gradually stretched the meaning of the 1962 Kennedy-Khrushchev accord. In 1970 the Soviets quietly attempted to build a submarine servicing base at Cienfuegos, Cuba. On 9 September a Soviet squadron arrived at Cay Alcatrez in the Bay of Cienfuegos. It included an oceangoing tug, a ship with two special purpose barges (used to support nuclear submarines), and a submarine tanker. The arrival of the squadron prompted a U-2 surveillance mission that revealed the construction of a naval facility. The Soviets backed down when the United States vigorously protested. In mid-November the United States announced an "understanding" with the Soviets concerning the prohibition of servicing nuclear-armed submarines in Cuban ports.

As if to underscore this determination to restrain Soviet influence in the Caribbean, the United States in July 1971 organized Destroyer Squadron 18, which exercised surveillance over Soviet naval activity around Cuba. In the spring of 1972 the Soviets tested the so-called Cienfuegos understandings by quietly sending a Golf-II, diesel-powered, ballistic-missile-equipped submarine and a submarine tender into the Cuban port of Nipe. As in other instances of Soviet naval visits to Cuba, Squadron 18 was anchored six miles off the coast and later tracked the submarine when it left port—until, that is, Soviet ships engaged in close maneuvers around the U.S. ships, forcing them to break sonar contact with the submarine. Still, the submarine had been repeatedly forced to surface until the fleet had gone some distance.[1]

The Soviets had selected an opportune time to test the limits of the "understandings," for when the Soviet submarine was at Nipe President Nixon was planning to visit Moscow in three weeks for a summit conference and the signing of the Strategic Arms Limitations Treaty (SALT I). Obviously U.S. officials were expected not to jeopardize this triumph of Nixonian foreign policy. The incident was not publicized or protested.

In July 1973 Squadron 18 was decommissioned, and the navy terminated use of Key West as a base. From 1970 the Soviets gradually escalated their military activities in and around Cuba. During the summer of 1970 the Soviet Union began to send occasional flights of TU-95 Bear reconnaissance aircraft from Murmansk (in the northwest of the republic of Russia) to Cuba over the north Atlantic. In September 1972, however, operational reconnaissance flights began on a regular basis to establish the practice of routine patrol. The aircraft would fly from Cuban bases, head up the east coast of the United States, past Cape Canaveral and U.S. Navy facilities, and return to Cuba.

The United States did not challenge these flights, in part because the Soviets were careful not to use the bomber or cruise-missile versions of the TU-95. The navy was aware of this new Soviet surveillance from Cuba, but the public was not. By 1977 these bombers were patrolling very close to the coast of the United States and conducting surveillance missions over all fleet and space-program activities in the waters adjacent to the United States. The number and strength of Soviet Naval visits to Cuba increased, and by 1975 ballistic-missile submarines were routinely using Cuban ports. In May 1979 the Soviets gave the Cuban navy its first two submarines. Some in the U.S. Navy believed that the Soviets were "trying to build an elephant a little at a time."[2]

U.S. influence and prestige underwent a serious decline from the late 1960s through the 1970s, and this was reflected in the Caribbean role of the nation. The ignominious retreat from Vietnam had been capped by the complete destruction by the North Vietnamese of the Paris Peace Accords, negotiated by Henry Kissinger, and the final conquest of South Vietnam. The United States betrayed its Vietnamese allies and was not even given the benefit of a dignified withdrawal from Saigon. When General Omar Torrijos of Panama made some belligerent declarations about taking over the canal, someone asked him if he were not afraid of the U.S. Army. He replied that he was not afraid of U.S. soldiers "because they are the same as those who stampeded out of Vietnam."[3]

U.S. international prestige took another beating from the political debacle of the Nixon administration. First, Vice President Spiro Agnew was forced to resign in October 1973 under charges of corruption. Then the Watergate scandal broke in early 1973, and for the next 15 months President Nixon's primary attention was given to defending himself. For the first time since 1867 the Senate Judiciary Committee began hearings on impeachment. The climax came in early August 1974, when Nixon resigned the presidency. By this time the executive branch was in shambles and U.S. prestige badly battered.

In addition, during the 1970s the Congress was hard at work slashing the military. By the latter part of the decade some navy ships were going to sea half-manned, and many pilots in the interceptor command were flying airplanes older than themselves. Certainly the Soviets considered this overall decline in U.S. military strength significant, as the heightened Soviet military activity in the Caribbean and other parts of the world attests. As Arkady N. Shevchenko, the highest-ranking Soviet official ever to defect, stated, "By 1975 . . . Moscow was welcoming and encouraging Cuba's adventurism." As he explained, this was based on the assessment by Soviet leaders that the power of the United States was rapidly declining owing to the internal decay of the capitalist system.[4]

When Jimmy Carter became president in 1977 he made Washington more accessible to the left wing of the Democratic party. This element had grown in numbers and influence since the mid-1960s and embodied a crusading mentality aimed at all right-wing regimes. Those on the party's left had assumed the hair shirt of American guilt. In atonement, they were willing to accept a variety of demands made by the more radical third-world spokesmen. Within the new Carter administration there was opposition to the left, but for about two years it exercised considerable influence over Latin American and African policy making in the State Department. This impetus had some of its roots in Congress and had already been demonstrated by congressional action cutting off all aid to South Vietnam in 1973, the War Powers Act (November 1973), and the Clark Amendment to the Defense Appropriations Act of January 1976 that prevented the United States from aiding Jonas Savimbi's anti-Communist guerrilla forces in Angola.

For almost three years the Carter State Department displayed an affinity for left-wing regimes, and overtures were made to Fidel Castro to improve U.S.-Cuban relations. The Carter administration essentially viewed any government to the left as "good" and believed that the United States must support all groups claiming to be revolutionary. Leading U.S. Senators of the Democratic left (George McGovern and Frank Church) were given tours of Cuba (complete with cigars and khaki field caps) and received the blessings of Castro. On their return, the Senators praised the Castro regime, noting that under Castro the peasants ran on time, even if Castro's motorcade did not. The United States' U.N. ambassador, Andrew Young, praised the stabilizing effects of Cuban military intervention in Angola, and early in 1977 Carter terminated all flights of spy planes over Cuba. In addition, the administration granted visas for some Cubans to enter the United States, dropped restrictions on U.S. citizens wanting to travel to Cuba, negotiated the opening of diplomatic interest sections in both nations, and further modified the U.S. trade embargo. The United States and Cuba signed provisional maritime boundary and fishing rights agreements in April 1977, and charter flights between the two countries were started.

To accommodate the human-rights argument, Castro released several American political prisoners and permitted all American citizens still in Cuba to go to the U.S. with all members of their households. Late in 1978 Castro announced that he would release almost all political prisoners and allow them to leave Cuba. By November 1979 some 3,600 had been released. Some authorities argued that this was only a portion of Castro's prisoners. The Cuban premier, however, refused to discuss the Cuban military role in Africa.

Nicaragua presented the left wing of the Carter administration with the perfect opportunity to test one of its oldest dogmas—the belief that Marxist-oriented regimes became unfriendly to the United States and turned to Moscow for support only because they were provoked by a hostile United States. In other words, the Democratic left believed the United States was solely to blame for any anti-U.S. feeling or actions in the world.

The Sandinista National Liberation Front launched an all-out attack on the Somoza regime in 1978, and the U.S. government not only cut off its own military aid to Somoza but prevented others from providing such assistance. Cuban military advisers of the Department of Special Operations aided in the coordination of the war effort, and Cuba also helped to organize, train, and transport an "international brigade" to fight in Nicaragua. The regime collapsed, and the Sandinistas seized power in July 1979. Although members of the directorate were generally Marxist in orientation, they had formed a broad coalition to defeat Somoza, and in the beginning the Nicaraguan revolution seemed to be following an independent course. Castro advised the Sandinistas to proceed slowly so as not to antagonize the United States or drive out the skilled professionals too quickly, and the United States immediately afforded emergency assistance to the Sandinistas worth some $8 million.[5] This consisted of foodstuffs, medicines, tents, blankets, and other items. On 30 August the two countries signed an agreement providing for $2.9 million in food shipments. Despite some congressional opposition, the Carter administration also pushed through a measure providing for additional economic assistance. In 1979 the administration asked for a 1980 budget of $75 million for economic assistance for Nicaragua (the entire Caribbean–Central American aid request was for $80 million). The official policy statement of the administration declared that the U.S. approach in Nicaragua was "one of friendly cooperation, with effective and timely economic and humanitarian aid."[6]

But beginning in late 1979 the Carter administration's flirtation with Marxist-Leininst regimes began to unravel. In September the United States announced the discovery of a Soviet combat brigade (about 2,500 men) in Cuba and declared this to be a violation of the Kennedy-Khrushchev accord. The brigade consisted of one tank and three infantry battalions with 40 tanks and 60 armored personnel carriers. The Soviets rejected the U.S. protests and claimed that the unit was a "training center." After three weeks of negotiations the Soviets in effect told the Carter administration where to go, and the semicrisis ended in a whimper. Carter declared that surveillance of Cuba would be increased, a permanent full-time Caribbean Task Force Headquarters would be established in Key West, and that military maneuvers in the Caribbean would be expanded. Unfortunately, the administration had been steadily cutting the navy's budget, and some ships, as noted earlier, were only 50 percent manned.

To add to Carter's growing disillusionment, on 4 November 1979 the fanatical hordes of the Mullah Ayatollah Khomeini in Iran seized the U.S. Embassy and took some 63 hostages. Then the Soviet Union invaded Afghanistan in December 1979. The Soviets supported Iran, and their clandestine radio stations urged the Iranians to increase their anti-American crusade. After Afghanistan, the president lamented that he had learned a lot about communism while in office.

As if to add insult to injury, Castro turned a political liability and embarrassent into a major problem for Carter. In April 1980 a group of Cubans, desperate to leave the island, managed to break into the Peruvian Embassy compound. Castro's first reaction was to crack down, but he reversed himself and announced that all could leave who so desired. When thousands of Cubans, including blacks and young people, lined up for permission to leave, Castro suffered some embarrassment. He then literally pushed these people out by loading them on numerous small boats and aiming them at the United States. Of course, Cubans in the United States came with boats in the hope of picking up relatives, but without any organization a flood of over 125,000 Cubans poured into south Florida. Castro opened his jails and mental institutions and used the boatlift as a method of unloading his undesirables. Some of those in jail were political prisoners, such as the poets Reinaldo Arenas and Roberto Valero, so being an "undesirable" in Cuba did not necessarily mean that one was a criminal. The sorting out and settling of this horde now became Carter's dilemma.

The Nicaraguan Sandinistas adopted an increasingly pro-Soviet, anti-U.S. posture during 1980. The regime began to crack down on those who dissented (including the anti-Somoza newspaper *La Prensa*) and to build one of the largest armies in Latin America. As early as August 1979 five Soviet generals visited Nicaragua to begin the creation of the new army. U.S. offers to help train a new army were rejected. Increasing numbers of Cuban, East German, and Soviet advisers moved in, and the Soviets began to send T-55 tanks and MIG fighter planes as well. According to some intelligence reports, the Cubans were sending combat military units by late 1980.[7]

As if to underscore the kind of relations with the United States they wanted, the Sandinistas adopted a national anthem containing the words "The United States is the enemy of mankind." But the Carter administration was most provoked by the flow of arms and equipment from Cuba, through Nicaragua, to the Marxist guerrillas in El Salvador. In addition, in 1980 the Cubans stepped up training of Salvadoran guerrillas. This led President Carter to order military assistance for El Salvador.

Carter had begun his administration with ringing statements about the end of the cold war. By the time he left office in 1981, after an overwhelming defeat in November 1980, much had changed. He now realized that the Soviet-Cuban concept of detente simply meant that there would be peaceful relations *if* the United States accepted its role as a "has-been" power, withdrew to the sidelines of world affairs, and left a clear field for the spread of

Soviet power and areas of control. The Caribbean–Central American region seemed to reflect this development. Nicaragua was only one aspect. In March 1979 Maurice Bishop's New Jewel Movement seized control of the island of Grenada (one of the windward islands) and oriented the country toward Cuba and the Soviet Union in both domestic and international affairs. The Cubans, with Soviet equipment, began construction of a major airfield on the island. Bishop proclaimed its potential for the tourist trade, yet the 9,800-foot main runway would accommodate every military aircraft in the Soviet-Cuban inventory. Jamaica also was moving toward Castroism until the election of November 1980, when Edward Seaga became prime minister and reversed this policy. But in various other Central American–Caribbean countries, the Cubans, with Soviet support, were stepping up their efforts to arm, train, and coordinate guerrilla activities.

When he became president in 1981 Ronald Reagan inherited this mess of expanding guerrilla warfare, economic distress, and political turmoil in the circum-Caribbean region. For the first time in several years the term *Monroe Doctrine* was used by U.S. officials, and the new administration promised a much tougher approach toward Cuban-Soviet actions in the Western Hemisphere. In February 1981 the United States stopped most aid to Nicaragua, and during the year President Reagan stepped up the flow of arms and equipment to El Salvador. The number of Special Forces advisors sent to the country was frozen at 55, and they were restricted to carrying only the .45 automatic service pistol. The latter restriction was changed after several advisors were killed in defensive operations. In addition, Salvadoran officers and NCOs were brought to the United States for training.

In 1981 El Salvador became a very emotional issue as the left in the United States and Europe orchestrated a campaign to condemn the Salvadoran government led by José Napoleon Duarte, a Christian Democrat. The campaign was bolstered by the viciousness of the war and by the well-publicized atrocities of the extreme right-wing National Guard—especially the murder of four American Churchwomen in 1980. The atrocities of the left-wing guerrillas received relatively little media coverage, however, and statements of Salvadoran church leaders attacking the guerrillas were also ignored.[8] The *Boston Globe* ran a series of interviews with the guerrillas, however, that undermined their supporters' claims that Cuba and Nicaragua were not involved. One commander stated that eventually they would be fighting in Mexico, and that the ultimate target was the United States.[9]

The Reagan administration attempted to negotiate with Nicaragua and Cuba concerning their supplying arms to the guerrillas in El Salvador. The leaders of these countries—Castro included—denied the allegations in public but admitted their truth in private.[10] The assistant secretary for inter-American affairs visited Nicaragua in August 1981 and tried to arrange a deal whereby the United States would guarantee not to support the rebels attacking Nicaragua if the Sandinistas would stop funneling arms into El Salvador. The latter rejected any deal but continued to charge that the United States was trying to overthrow the Nicaraguan regime and even planning to invade that country with Marines. In early 1982 the United States tried again to stop the flow of arms by peaceful means. Secret talks were held with Cuban and Nicaraguan leaders, but these produced no results.

Cuba's expanded efforts to overthrow governments in Latin America and create pro-Soviet regimes in their place had other repercussions. In March 1981 a group of guerrillas trained and supplied by Cuba launched an attack in Colombia, but the peasants refused to support them and the "revolution" was smashed. The president of Colombia broke relations with Cuba, thus reversing a trend that had been running since the early 1970s. Two days later the government of Panama announced that it was reconsidering relations with Cuba because of its policy of exporting violence. In addition, Cuban-backed guerrillas in Guatemala became more active.

In 1981 the Soviets vastly increased their shipments of arms to Cuba, sending the largest amount since the Missile Crisis of 1962. The number of surveillance missions over U.S. Navy operations flown out of Cuba by Soviet Tu-5 "Bear D" planes also increased. The Soviets continued to send large shipments of arms to Nicaragua and to train Nicaraguan pilots in Cuba and Bulgaria. By 1982 the Cubans had sent approximately 2,000 military and security advisers to Nicaragua and (with Soviet assistance) were building four airfields. Commandante Cero (Eden Pastora), a Sandinista hero, broke with the regime and, after getting out of the country, denounced Soviet control over it. He also attacked the government's persecution of the Miskito Indians.

In 1981 President Reagan repeatedly warned Cuba and the Soviet Union that the United States was prepared to take all necessary measures to curb the flow of arms from Cuba and stop the spread of their military activities in the Caribbean. When asked what this entailed the president replied, "I rule nothing out, nothing in."[11] Yet, as of mid-1982, the president had acted very cautiously. The rhetoric had been strong, but aside from traditional military assistance programs, a few advisers in El Salvador, and the December 1981 upgrading of the Key West headquarters as a new U.S. military command for the Caribbean, President Reagan had pursued a rather pacifistic policy.

As if to underscore his peaceful efforts, the president announced his Caribbean Basin Initiative on 24 February 1982. In an address to the OAS he presented a program to help stimulate economic development in the region. The plan called for preferential, duty-free treatment for almost all Caribbean exports to the United States, tax incentives for American businesses investing in the area, increased technical assistance and training, and $350 million in supplemental aid for fiscal year 1982. Of this, $135 million would be earmarked for El Salvador—$100 million for economic assistance and $35 million in military aid. In addition, Reagan called on Venezuela and Mexico to participate in these development efforts. The initiative became bogged down in Congress, however, owing to opposition to removing duties from some Caribbean products.

In October 1983 the United States struck back at the growing Soviet incursion into the Caribbean. When Maurice Bishop and a band of 40 overthrew the government of Grenada, which had held power since independence in 1974, the people of this small island were propelled into the arena of cold war power politics. Bishop, who has been described by Georgie Anne Geyer as a "romantic revolutionary," wanted to follow in the footsteps of his long-time idol Fidel Castro.[12] Like Castro, Bishop had ousted an unpopular dictator and could bask in the afterglow of this success even though the New Jewel Movement created its own totalitarian regime. For Castro, the new government provided something he had lacked in the past—access to the English-speaking Caribbean.

The Cubans, with East German assistance, not only began construction of the Point Salines airfield but also started work on a naval base at Egmont Harbor, two and a half miles north of Point Salines. The harbor is considered to be one of the best protected anchorages in the southern Caribbean. Grenadan officials routinely denied that either facility had any military purpose, but Selwyn Strachan, minister of mobilization, did state publicly that Cuba would be able to use the new airport to supply its troops in Africa and that the Soviets would also find it useful owing to its "strategic location." In 1980 Grenada signed a treaty with the Soviets giving them landing rights for Tu-95 reconnaissance aircraft.[13] Approximately 56 percent of all oil imported into the United States came through tanker lanes or was produced by refineries within a 500-mile radius of Grenada.

The New Jewel government wanted to be accepted as full allies of the Soviet Union, not as just a Cuban dependency. As the Grenadan ambassador to the Soviet Union explained, "Our revolution has to be viewed as a worldwide process with its original roots in the Great October Revolution. For Grenada to assume a position of increasingly greater importance, we have to be seen as influencing at least regional events. We have to establish ourselves as the authority on events in at least the English-speaking Caribbean, and be the sponsor of revolutionary activity and progressive developments in this region at least." The ambassador believed that Surinam (formerly Dutch Guiana) was the "most likely candidate for special attention." He noted, "If we can be an overwhelming influence on Surinam's international behavior, then our importance in the Soviet scheme of things will be greatly enhanced. To the extent we can take credit for bringing any other country into the progressive fold, our prestige and influence would be greatly enhanced."[14]

By mid-1983 Grenada's government had signed agreements with the Soviet Union, Vietnam, Czechoslovakia, North Korea, Cuba, and East Germany for both military equipment and technical logistical assistance. Grenada received enough arms to equip a 10,000-man army and planned to place as much as 15 to 20 percent of the population under arms. For an island of 89,000 people this would have come close to being the largest army, in proportion to population, in the world. In addition to receiving thousands of small arms, Grenada received 82-mm mortars, a 75-mm cannon, armored personnel carriers, antiaircraft guns, and 75 trucks from East Germany. Grenada also requested loudspeakers, 2,000 folding chairs, and four guillotines.[15]

The Vietnamese had begun to train Grenadans in the methods of setting up so-called reeducation camps to deal with those who did not accept the Communist order (as had been done in South Vietnam) and in dealing with "Yankee tactics and weapons."[16] The Soviet KGB had been requested to supply personnel to train a secret police force.

The Soviet Union gladly embraced its new ally in the Western Hemisphere. In March 1983 Marshall Nikolai V. Ogarkov, chief of staff of the Soviet army, and other high-ranking officers met with Major Einstein Louison chief of staff of the Grenadan army who was studying at a Soviet military school in Moscow, and told him that "over two decades ago there was only Cuba in Latin America, today there are Nicargaua, Grenada and a serious battle is going on in El Salvador. The Marshall of the Soviet Union then stressed that United States imperialism would try to prevent progress but that there were no prospects for imperialism to turn back history." Marshall Ogarkov assured Major Louison that Soviet specialists would soon be sent "to conduct studies related to the construction of military projects." They concluded the meeting with a toast, "for the growth and further strengthening of the relations between the Soviet Armed Forces and the People's Revolutionary Armed Forces of Grenada."[17]

One of the construction projects to which Ogarkov referred was a new port and a cement plant on the island of Carriacou, an 11-square mile dependency north of Grenada and adjacent to St. Vincent and the Grenadines. The harbor would be constructed at Tyrrel Bay, a sheltered anchorage that had been used by the British fleet in the eighteenth century.[18]

President Reagan and his advisors were convinced that the growing Soviet presence in the Caribbean had to be stopped, and even reversed. The Reagan administration hoped this could be done peacefully, but Cuba was the key to any peaceful resolution, as it was the main base and supply point for all Soviet operations. And Cuba played the surrogate role for the Soviets even though Castro saw it as a leadership role. In 1982 President Reagan sent General Vernon Walters on a secret mission to Castro to find out if he wanted a peaceful deal. Walters, a CIA veteran and U.S. ambassador to the United Nations, spoke fluent Spanish but, after an evening of repartee and serious discussion, left Cuba convinced that Castro's hatred for the United States made any effective arrangements impossible. Castro, it was later reported by a diplomat, respected Walters but said that he had a "great defect"—"He would not let me talk."[19]

The failure of the Walters mission convinced Reagan that direct action would be needed to stop the spread of Soviet power in the Caribbean. The time, place, and circumstances would have to be chosen carefully owing to the fact that many Democrats were wary of another Vietnam situation. The needed factors came together in October 1983 on the island of Grenada.

A group of fanatic Marxist-Leninists, led by Bernard Coard, decided that the easy-going Bishop was not moving with enough determination to solidify the Communist state and that he might even be considering improving relations with the United States. A power struggle resulted that culminated in Bishop's arrest. On 19 October his followers freed him, but Coard and the army seized him, and in the courtyard of Fort Rupert Bishop and a number of his associates were literally blown away by machine-gun fire. An unknown number of others were killed and wounded when the army opened fire on a crowd of citizens. Some reports stated that the Soviet ambassador, General Gennadiy I. Sazhenev, directed the coup and gave his approval for the execu

This poster, distributed by the New Jewel Movement (NJM), exemplifies Grenada's close ties with Cuba and Nicaragua. *Left to right:* Daniel Ortega, Maurice Bishop, and Fidel Castro. Source: Department of State and Department of Defense, *The Soviet-Cuban Connection in Central America and the Caribbean,* March 1985, 4.

tions.[20] Grenadan General Hudson Austin took control, decreed a 24-hour curfew for four days, and declared that anyone found on the streets would be shot on sight.

On 20 October the seven member islands of the Organization of Eastern Caribbean States met and decided that their security was in jeopardy. Prime Minister John Compton of St. Lucia took the lead in calling for intervention by a multinational force. Very quickly the island leaders decided to invite the United States, Barbados, and Jamaica to assist. In part, their action was precipitated when the governor-general of Grenada, Sir Paul Scoon, sent them a confidential appeal for assistance to restore order.

In addition, some 700 American students were attending a medical school on the island and there was some concern for their safety. The coup leaders assured the administration of St. George's Medical School that the students were in no danger. The students themselves believed that they were. One student later said of President Reagan, "He really did save our lives."[21] And, with the memory of the Iranian hostage crisis still fresh, there were officials who did not want to risk a repetition.

In any event, the combination of the military coup and its attendent violence, martial law, and canceling of commercial flights left the American students in a potentially dangerous situation. Thus the invitation to intervene presented the Reagan administration with the time, place, and circumstances to strike at a Soviet ally. It is doubtful that armed intervention had been seriously contemplated at any time before the coup, as there was no evidence of serious prior planning during the military operation.

On the morning of 25 October 1983 the United States launched Operation Urgent Fury. The element of surprise was not achieved since the Grenadans had been alerted by persons in some governmental capacity in the United States. Almost from its beginning, the operation was characterized by confusion and lack of coordination. Virtually every element in the U.S. military played a role: air force, navy, army (82nd Airborne), Marines, Army Rangers, Navy Seals, and Delta Force personnel. If the Los Angeles Police Department had requested a role, they probably would have gotten a piece of the action. The lack of advance planning and intelligence data quickly became evident, which was further complicated by the resistance of some 800 Cubans and an indeterminate number of Grenadans. For example, the Marines had British maps while some army units had to improvise with Michelin road maps. The night before the attack army personnel drew grid coordinates on the road maps—the only problem was that these differed from the Marine grid, which produced casualties from "friendly fire." Each of the four services used different radio frequencies for controlling air to ground strikes, and army and marine units could not communicate. When army units wanted support from aircraft carriers they had to call Ft. Bragg in North Carolina and have the message relayed via satellite to the navy commander, who passed it along to the air controller aboard a carrier. Owing to bureaucratic confusion, a number of C-130 transports were diverted from Ft. Stewart to Ft. Bragg, and two-thirds of the rangers were left sitting on the runway. The remaining one-third had to jump from 500 feet (many without reserve chutes) because the small Delta

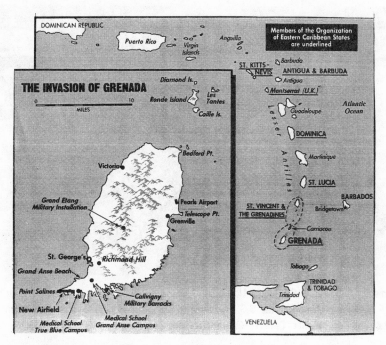

THE INVASION OF GRENADA

0   10
MILES

DOMINICAN REPUBLIC

Puerto Rico

Virgin Islands

Anguilla

Members of the Organization of Eastern Caribbean States are underlined

ST. KITTS-NEVIS

Barbuda

ANTIGUA & BARBUDA

Antigua

Montserrat (U.K.)

Guadeloupe

Atlantic Ocean

DOMINICA

Martinique

ST. LUCIA

BARBADOS

ST. VINCENT & THE GRENADINES

Bridgetown

Carriacou

GRENADA

Tobago

TRINIDAD & TOBAGO

Trinidad

VENEZUELA

Diamond Is.

Ronde Island

Les Tantes

Caille Is.

Bedford Pt.

Victoria

Grand Etang Military Installation

Pearls Airport

Telescope Pt.

Grenville

St. George's

Richmond Hill

Grand Anse Beach

Point Salines

New Airfield

Calivigny Military Barracks

Medical School True Blue Campus

Medical School Grand Anse Campus

Map of the Caribbean and Lesser Antilles and (inset) showing the October 1983 invasion of Grenada. © 1983 the *Washington Post.* Reprinted by permission.

Force had not been able to clear the runway at Point Salines. The latter suffered 22 casualties (not acknowledged, as the force "did not exist") after being surrounded by Cubans.[22]

The students at the True Blue campus next to the airport were rescued at about 9 A.M., but the rangers found out that a larger number of students were at the Grand Anse campus, about four miles away. The 82nd Airborne drove toward that objective and, with assistance from the rangers, secured that campus by late afternoon. By the middle of 27 October the operation was pretty much over. It was a victory, but the attack was neither swift nor surgical. Grenada was secure, but the American military still had a lot of work to do to overcome the effects of the budget bashing of the 1970s.[23] All in all, some 7,300 U.S. military personnel took part along with 300 police from Jamaica, Barbados, and St. Lucia.

Casualty figures are subject to question. The United States acknowledged the death of 18 and wounding of 116, but these figures do not include special forces. If these are included the killed-in-action figure rises to 29 and the wounded to at least 152. The U.S. government also listed the Grenadan casualty figures as 45 killed (21 military personnel) and 337 wounded. When a newspaper questioned these figures, the number killed was raised to 67 and wounded to 368. Twenty-four Cubans were killed and 59 wounded.[24]

The success of the Grenada operation infuriated and embarrassed Fidel Castro. General Rafael del Pino, the highest-ranking Cuban defector, has reported that Castro assembled his military leaders and ordered them to prepare aircraft to attack the United States. The objective was the Turkey Point

American students at St. George University, Grenada, surround an American soldier after his arrival at the campus with the U.S.-Caribbean forces, October 1983. Source: Department of State and Department of Defense, *Grenada: A Preliminary Report*, 16 December 1983, 4.

nuclear power plant south of Miami. He was probably dissuaded by the information that the radioactive fallout would do Cuba more damage than the United States.[25]

Twenty-four hours before the launching of Urgent Fury Castro had sent Colonel Pedro Tortolo Comas and between 150 and 200 combat troops to Grenada to prepare for an American attack—and to die fighting. When the veterans of Grenada stepped, or were carried, off the planes at Havana airport, Castro slouched in the background—silent for a change. Colonel Tortolo was demoted to private, sent to Angola, and reportedly killed.[26]

The U.S. intervention produced a mixed reaction. Some of its allies, including Great Britain, joined in a U.N. resolution condemning it. In the United States the Congressional Black Caucus condemned the operation, although 60 percent of blacks surveyed approved. Some Democratic leaders gave their support after visiting the island and seeing the physical evidence (documents, weapons, etc.) of the Soviet-Cuban presence.[27]

A survey conducted on Trinidad and Tobago revealed that 63 percent believed that force was the only alternative, 61 percent agreed that U.S. participation was justified, and 56 percent believed that the government of Trinidad and Tobago should have joined the invasion. A survey of the people of Grenada showed that 86 percent of the population favored intervention. In fact, some five years later one could still find such slogans on walls in Grenada as "Reagan: Hero of the World" and "USA Stay."[28]

President Reagan's favorite analysis of Urgent Fury came fron Lieutenant John P. De Hart, a Marine Corps Cobra pilot. De Hart noted that every story about Grenada contained something about the island producing more nutmeg than any other place on earth, and he decided that this was a code for the real reason why the United States intervened. As the officer wrote, "Number one,

Grenada produces more nutmeg than anyplace in the world. Number two, the Soviets and the Cubans are trying to take Grenada. Number three, you can't make good eggnog without nutmeg. Number four, you can't have Christmas without eggnog. Number five, the Soviets and Cubans are trying to steal Christmas. Number six, we stopped them."[29]

By 15 December 1983 all U.S. combat troops had left the island. Some 270 military personnel, along with some CPF troops from Jamaica, Barbados, and St. Lucia, remained to help the Grenadans keep order and build a police force. Army engineers also helped to repair damaged facilities and roads. U.S. economic assistance flowed to the island, and AID immediately dispatched medicine, food, water tanks, electrical generators and other emergency items. Rehabilitation projects were created in areas such as water supply, electric power, sewage disposal, and road repair. Both the United States and Canada provided funds to complete the Point Salines airfield. Congress approved $15 million for economic development in November 1983 and in 1984 approved an AID fund of $57 million. An interim government was set up by Governor-General Scoon in December 1983, and elections were held in December 1984. As a result of elections held in the spring of 1990, Nicholas Brathwaite became the country's first elected prime minister.

The success of Operation Urgent Fury sent a chill through Sandinista leaders in Nicaragua and the guerrillas in El Salvador. The Sandinistas believed that it was a dress rehearsal for an invasion of Nicaragua by the "crazy cowboy" in the White House. The Soviets and Cubans told them that in case of a U.S. attack they could not expect any military assistance. As a result, in late 1983 the Sandinistas curtailed both the training of Salvadoran guerrillas and arms shipments. They hoped to buy time until their network in the United States and their congressional contacts could stir up opposition to any U.S. intervention.

For a time the Sandinista strategy of manipulating U.S. opinion and congressional policy seemed to be working. Thus the Nicaraguans resumed the training of guerrillas and the shipment of arms not only to guerrillas in El Salvador but also to those in Costa Rica and Guatemala. The Soviet Union increased its shipment of arms, supplying tanks (some 250 by 1986), artillery, and attack helicopters. Major Roger Miranda Bengoechea, who served as the top aide to Nicaraguan Defense Minister Humberto Ortega before defecting in late 1987, reported that the Soviets had agreed to support a massive military buildup aimed at destroying the anti-Communist guerrillas—the so-called contras—and then to support the Communist guerrillas in Guatemala, El Salvador, Honduras, and Costa Rica. Miranda cited a total figure of 500,000 active and reserve soldiers as the goal, but in a speech the defense minister said the figure was 600,000.[30]

In late 1981 the Reagan administration had approved aid for a variety of anti-Communist guerrilla groups. In December 1984 some Democrats in Congress tried to hamstring these efforts without directly supporting the Sandinistas, and the Nicaraguans played a shrewd game of manipulating these fence sitters. The five Boland Amendments—sponsored by Representative Edward Boland of Massachusetts—were successive steps in this effort aimed at "encumbering but not killing the President's program." As Richard Perle, the former assistant secretary of defense, further explained, "For the Congress, it was far better to put less than a half a tank of gas in the President's car and leave it to *him* to explain why *his* policy never made it home."[31] Amendment No. 3 (passed in October 1984) specified that no government funds could be spent on behalf of the contras by the CIA, the Defense Department, or agencies "involved in intelligence activities." Amendment No. 5 (passed in November 1985) allowed the United States to obtain contra aid from third countries.

Whether congressional Democrats went to such lengths to support the Communist regime in Nicaragua because of their affinity for left-wing politics or their desire to set an Andrew Johnson type impeachment trap for Ronald Reagan is not entirely clear. What is clear is that Lieutenant Colonel Oliver North (U.S. Marine Corps) and other members of the National Security Council devised an elaborate and complex scheme to, in effect, kill two birds with one stone. A plan to sell certain types of missiles to Iran in return for Iranian cooperation in freeing American hostages held in Lebanon was expanded into a plan to use the profits from the sales to fund arms shipments to the Nicaraguan anti-Communist resistance. Colonel North believed that this transaction was legal because the Defense Department was paid in full (with some profit) and the actual "diversion" of profits to the contras was done by the arms sales middlemen (in effect turning over part of their own rather large profit). Richard Perle has provided a logical summary of what became the Iran-contra affair. He notes that the Boland restrictions were enacted with "a wink and a nod." A wink at the law and a nod in the direction of what in Washington is known as a "workaround." In this case, the workaround was entrusted to Colonel North, who discharged his assignments with a passion that, for all its excesses and failures of judgments, was admirably dedicated and undoubtedly selfless.[32]

Whatever one thinks of the legality or wisdom of the Iran-contra affair, the executive branch has been devising ways to work around Congress since 1810 when the "secret service fund" was created. In 1844 this fund was used by Secretary of State Daniel Webster to pay off newspaper editors and politicians in Maine to secure their support for the Maine boundary provisions of the Webster-Ashburton Treaty. In 1919 the State Department "illegally" diverted funds into a phony account to pay for Herbert O. Yardley's cryptographic (code-breaking) center known as the Black Chamber, and in 1920 the Navy Department did the same to pay for counter-intelligence operations that included breaking into the Japanese Consulate in New York. Franklin D. Roosevelt secretly diverted funds to pay for the combat operations of the Flying Tigers against the Japanese in China—an act of war since the two countries were still at peace. The Iran-contra affair stemmed from a long historical tradition that cut across party lines. Even Thomas Jefferson believed that at times the president had to protect the country by breaking laws enacted by ill-informed or malevolent Congressmen.

Then in June 1986 Congress approved $700 million in military aid and $30 million in nonlethal aid for the anti-Communist resistance, even though the speaker of the house, Thomas "Tip" O'Neil, deliberately delayed the legislation for four months. In late 1987 Congress approved more funds for arms, and the president ordered the resumption of CIA airdrops of arms to the contras.

When the Nicaraguan army attacked resistance bases along the Honduran border in March 1988, Reagan dispatched four battalions of U.S. troops from the 82nd Airborne Division and the 7th Light Infantry to Honduras with the implied threat that Nicaraguan forces had better leave Honduran soil. Nicaraguan President Daniel Ortega said that Reagan was acting like Superman, and noted that "Superman was defeated in Vietnam." Yet these forces quickly evacuated Honduras.

Meanwhile, the contras were increasing in strength to more than 20,000 and were becoming more proficient. Most were young peasants, male and female. The intensity of the Sandinista's losing efforts to defeat them can be deduced from Roger Miranda's information that by early 1987 the Sandinistas had consumed their entire 1985–90 allotment of Soviet-bloc weapons and ammunition and had to negotiate an increase.[33]

In mid-1987 the president of Costa Rica, Oscar Arias, came out with a peace plan for Central America, and the U.S. Senate voted 97 to 1 to accept it. Thus began a yo-yo-like peace process that would go on for almost the next three years. After blowing hot and cold for several months, the Sandinistas signed the Sapoa Accords in March 1988, and the process of trying to democratize Nicaragua and plan free elections began. Then the U.S. House rejected an administration proposal to provide humanitarian assistance and possible new military aid to the anti-Communist forces.

With official aid to the anti-Communist guerrillas cut off by the U.S. Congress, the Sandinistas believed they could move back to a more totalitarian policy. In mid-1988 they cracked down on the opposition, arresting five of the main leaders. In October the U.S. ambassador and seven other officials were expelled, four labor and political leaders were murdered, and a nationwide state of emergency reimposed. When rumblings of protest were once more heard from the United States, the Sandinistas trooped back to the conference table, and in February 1989 the Costa Del Sol Accords were signed. These accords provided for elections in early 1990 and a package of reforms (including freeing a number of political prisoners), and they stipulated that the contras should be expelled from Honduras. The anti-Communists were skeptical of Daniel Ortega's promises, and one leader declared, "Whatever accord is reached based on Ortega's promise is equal to trying to leash a dog with sausages." To ease the process, George Bush, who became president in 1989, cut a deal with the Democrats and obtained for the anti-Communist forces $45 million in humanitarian aid, which was to be used over a 10-month period. Approval from four congressional committees would be required to continue such aid after 30 November 1989.

In 1989 the role of President Mikhail Gorbachev of the Soviet Union became increasingly important. At the time of his visit to Cuba in the spring of 1989 he was still trying to carry water on both shoulders—preaching glasnost and perestroika at home but doing little to actually cut down on Soviet military expenditures or involvement in the Caribbean. American officials had hoped that Gorbachev would offer restraint in supplying aid and weapons to Nicaragua, but he refused to make such a declaration and denounced the United States for aiding democracies in the area. He did offer a rather general condemnation of "exporting" revolution, but the signals were anything but clear. Perhaps the Soviet leader did inform the Nicaraguans that his internal economic problems might lead to a reduction in aid and thus they should humor the United States.

The Sandinistas kept up sporadic harassment of opposition election efforts throughout 1989. Plainclothes government goon squads, called *turbas*, attacked opposition rallies and killed several people at one of these in early December. The coalition opposition party (UNO) was allowed 30 minutes a day on the government-controlled television network, and Ortega declared that the Sandinistas, if defeated, would not give up power, only "shares of power." Forty-one former contras returned to Managua to participate in the elections. Twenty-seven were thrown in prison, and 12 were killed.

Then, in late December 1989, the United States intervened in Panama to overthrow General Manuel Noriega in Operation Just Cause. The economic embargo had failed to oust the strongman, who not only was deeply involved in aiding and abetting the drug trade between Colombia and the United States but had also threatened to destroy the Panama Canal Treaty and disrupt canal operations. Although Cuban-trained thugs, called "Dignity Battalions," prolonged the fighting and forced U.S. units to blast them out of civilian neighborhoods, few, if any, Panamanians followed Castro's prediction about going to the mountains to fight. Although the battalions fought for several days, the massacre planned by Castro and Noriega for the middle class did not take place.

Operation Just Cause proved that President George Bush was capable of forceful action. With the fall of the Berlin Wall and the collapse of Communist regimes in Eastern Europe, the Sandinistas faced a new set of international circumstances. The Soviet Union, beset by growing economic problems, was clearly on the defensive and could offer little, if any, support.

Thus the Sandinistas reduced their attacks on the UNO, and under the supervision of 2,000 U.N. observers free elections were held on 25 February 1990. The UNO won a stunning victory to the surprise and chagrin of the Sandinistas and their allies in the U.S. news media (who had been publicly predicting the exact opposite). The question at the time was, Would Ortega and company surrender power to the new president, Violeta Chamorro? There were some indications in March that the Sandinistas would not go peacefully. A deal was struck, however, and on 25 April 1990, the reins of power were handed over.

The official deal stated that the army and police were to be reduced and turned into "nonpartisan" organizations and that the contras were to be disarmed by a U.N. police force. It became apparent over the next few months that the army, although reduced in size and deprived of conscripts, still remained a Sandinista-controlled force. Humberto Ortega remained as defense minister with almost total control of the army, and the secret police were integrated into the army, with the same chief, Lenin Cerna. Marcos Arevalo, known as "The Butcher," remained as head of the prison system. In addition, the Sandinistas added 12,600 of their number to the public payroll after their defeat. President Chamorro has been unable to reduce the bloated, Sandinista-controlled public workforce, and her attempts brought massive strikes that threatened to topple the government unless she backed down. She did, and even granted huge pay raises despite the economic misery of her country.

By mid-1990 most of the contras had surrendered their arms and had moved into the special rural zones set aside in central and southern Nicaragua. In these areas they were supposed to police themselves and become part of the local governments.

Although eventually reduced to about 28,000 troops, the Sandinista army remained just that—not a Nicaraguan army. The army continued to supply troops and munitions to the Farabundo Marti National Liberation Front (FMLN) in El Salvador, and in March 1991 a truckload of munitions bound for that country was seized in Honduras. President Chamorro has kept her hands off army activities.

The Sandinistas had been looting Nicaragua for years, and this intensified after the election. The National Assembly in March 1990 had passed laws "legalizing" the massive seizure of property by Sandinistas. Some of this consisted of mansions and the estates of former Somoza officials. Daniel Ortega, for example, received title to a $500,000 mansion and made a token "purchase payment" of $4,000. Some 4,500 of the finer homes in Managua were turned over to Sandinista officials. Furthermore, these "friends of the poor" acquired large blocs of farmland. The former vice minister of agrarian reform, Ricardo Coronel, received the title to some 5,000 acres. By some estimates, the total value of the giveaway exceeded $1 billion.

In mid-1991 the Nicaraguan legislature took up a measure repealing the giveaways. The Sandinista legislators walked out, a number of bombings occurred, Sandinista mobs seized radio stations and government buildings, and Daniel Ortega declared that repeal could lead to war. Of course, the Sandinistas said that the proposed repeal would only hurt the urban squatters and rural peasants who supposedly had benefited from the property giveaways. In September President Chamorro vetoed the bill, which was modified to protect the rights of small owners and cooperatives. The end result was a standoff, and at the end of 1991 the new Marxist millionaires retained most of their holdings.

The United States has pledged over $541 million in economic aid and has delivered some $200 million. By the end of 1991 the country had received a total of $700 million from the United States and the European Community. As of 1993, however, Nicaragua is still sunk in the Sandinista-engineered depression. The economy had shrunk 50 percent under Sandinista socialism, and Nicaragua enjoyed the dubious distinction of passing Haiti to become the poorest country in Latin America.

On the bright side, the 13,500 percent rate of inflation, which occurred in 1990, has been cut to about 1 percent. The former guerrillas have given up their arms, but only about 9,461 have received the land they were promised. Sporadic violence still erupts in the rural areas, and in July 1993 a group of former Sandinista soldiers, calling themselves the Revolutionary Front of Workers and Peasants, attacked an army garrison in the northern city of Esteli. The army defeated this effort, but some 50 people were killed and more than 100 wounded. This left-wing group charged that the government had failed to make good on promises of land and credit for former soldiers. The re-contras struck in August in northern Nicaragua and seized a number of hostages, including parliamentary deputies and army officers. They demanded the resignation of several high-ranking officials, including Defense Minister General Humberto Ortega. Sandinista gunmen then took a number of hostages (including the vice president) in Managua. Cardinal Miguel Obando y Bravo negotiated the release of all hostages. Hostility still simmers, however, beneath the surface as more than 200 contras have been murdered during the past two years without any action on the part of the government.

Despite all the problems and the very slow progress being made in some areas, the people of Nicaragua enjoy more freedom than they have for many years. Democracy is still a most fragile plant, but it is surviving. Recently, the people of Los Goneadores voted to change the name of their village to Ronald Reagan because "he helped us a lot." Bernard Aronson, assistant secretary of state for inter-American affairs, wrote that "like other nations emerging from dictatorship in South America or Eastern Europe, Nicaragua's new democracy faces an uphill battle. . . . But given the difficulties, we believe Nicaragua merits our continued, active support."[34]

Yet the country no longer poses a strategic problem and its internal conflicts no longer seem to be of major importance in the broad spectrum of world problems. Perhaps a writer in a news magazine put it best, "The world is tired of Nicaragua, its endless crises and its bottomless tin cup. With the waning of the Cold War, the region's strategic or even tactical value to the superpowers has diminished greatly."[35]

Thanks to the same circumstances, the FMLN guerrillas began serious negotiations with the government of El Salvador. A special envoy from the United Nations acted as mediator in the December 1991 talks aimed at producing a formal cease-fire and finally an end to the conflict. On 1 January 1992 a formal agreement was reached between the government and the FMLN. A U.N. police force would supervise the cease-fire and implementation of the agreement. In October 1992 the United Nations announced that an agreement had been reached between the government and the rebels concerning land reform. Under this plan land would be distributed to some 15,000 government soldiers, 7,500 demobilized rebels, and 25,000 squatters. The announcement stated that the land-reform issue had been the last major obstacle to a conclusion of the civil war.

During the 1980s Cuba continued to provide the Soviet "foreign legion" in Africa. Some 250,000 Cubans were deployed. Castro dispatched an expeditionary force to Ethiopia, where the Cubans served under the command of a Soviet general. There were some 57,000 Cuban troops in Angola defending the Communist government, and between 5,000 to 7,000 in Ethiopia. Cuban detachments were sent to several other African countries, including Equatorial Guinea, Tanzania, Guinea Bissau, Algeria, Uganda, Sierra Leone, and Mozambique. In addition, thousands of Cuban troops could be found in Syria, North Korea, South Yemen, Libya, and elsewhere. Havana became one of the two largest guerrilla training centers in the world, as Castro actively supported some 27 guerrilla organizations around the world.

All of this could be accomplished only with Soviet support. Yet, during 1990, the problems of the Soviet and East European economies began to affect this support, as well as the massive subsidization of the Cuban economy. Soviet oil shipments fell about 24 percent, and various Eastern European nations began to demand hard currency for their meat, milk, grain, and manufactured goods. Cuba's economic situation became much worse in 1991. Direct Soviet grants, which had been over $4 billion a year, declined, and in December 1991 Castro announced that shipments of Soviet oil had stopped.

By the end of 1990 almost all items of food and clothing were severely rationed. Castro announced that Cuba was obtaining one million bicycles from China to replace vehicles and a new program to force thousands of Cubans to resettle in rural areas. He also declared Cuba was "opening up very wide" its economy to foreign investors for joint business ventures. Castro, of course, blamed the long-standing U.S. embargo for Cuba's economic ills, but in reality this had had little effect, as it applied only to U.S. companies. But even these—such as Cargill, Inc.—bypassed the embargo by using foreign subsidiaries.

All of these recent economic and international political complications forced Castro to make changes in his foreign activities. The Soviet Union had begun to curtail its African involvement in the late 1980s, and in 1989 Cuba agreed to a phased withdrawal of its troops from Angola. This was completed in 1991, and Cuban forces were also withdrawn from Ethiopia when that Communist regime was defeated.

Despite a Soviet retreat in Africa, Mikhail Gorbachev tried to hold on to his military ally in the Caribbean—one of the last elements of Soviet geopolitical influence. Despite U.S. pressure to remove the Soviet military presence in and ties to Cuba, Gorbachev stubbornly refused to do anything about the situation. In March 1991 a delegation to Cuba from the Supreme Soviet declared that there would be "no change" in areas related to defense or "joint activities."[36] Finally, in September 1991, after the failed coup attempt and Boris Yeltsin's rapid gain in influence, Gorbachev announced the gradual withdrawal of Soviet troops. But the Soviets later stressed that this withdrawal should be matched by corresponding steps from the United States, including a reduction in U.S. forces at Guantanamo Bay. Castro reacted angrily, but with the breakup of the Soviet Union the future of Soviet-Cuban relations was very much up in the air. Earlier in the year Czechoslovakia announced that it would no longer serve as Cuba's diplomatic representative in Washington. The Soviet force in Cuba at the end of 1991 included a 2,400-man motorized rifle brigade and some 4,000 advisers and communications specialists. The latter operated the electronic eavesdropping post at Lourdes outside Havana—a facility described as "the largest and most sophisticated intelligence collection site of its kind outside the U.S.S.R."[37] The future of this intelligence facility is unknown, but the Soviets have scaled back other military activities. There have been no reconnaissance flights since early 1990, and the last call made by a Soviet naval vessel at a Cuban port was June 1990.

Cuba also became involved in the smuggling of cocaine from Colombia into the United States by allowing overflights of planes and the use of Cuban ports and airfields. Castro has denied the charges and even had several high-ranking (and popular) officers executed for drug smuggling in 1989.

In September 1992 the United States took action to hasten the demise of the Castro regime and punish it for its increasing number of human-rights violations. The U.S. Congress enacted the Cuban Democracy Act of 1992, which was supported by the Bush administration and by presidential candidate Bill Clinton. The act provides that subsidiaries of American companies based abroad may be prosecuted if they do business with Cuba, and that ships trading with Cuba will be barred from U.S. ports for six months. In November 1992 the United Nations approved a resolution calling on all nations to reject the new embargo act. The vote was 59 to 3, with 71 countries abstaining. The first stage of the removal of Russian troops from Cuba began in late November 1992, when more than 870 soldiers and their family members departed on a cruise liner.

As president, Clinton appeared to switch positions. In June 1993 a delegation of former diplomatic and military officers went to Cuba to improve communications with the that country's government. The delegation was led by Wayne Smith, who had headed the U.S. diplomatic mission in Cuba during the Carter administration. In September the Cubans, for the first time, turned over to U.S. authorities two suspected drug smugglers and their boat. The head of the U.S. Drug Enforcement Agency, Robert Bonner, called this, "an important step forward in our bilateral counter-narcotic relationship."[38]

As president, Richard Nixon had to deal with a country he described as "a picture in poverty and pregnancy." One section of Governor Rockefeller's report in 1969 recommended that U.S. aid be restored to Haiti. The Inter-American Development Bank (IADB) granted a $5.5 million loan to expand the water supply for Port-au-Prince, but little else was done until after the death of François Duvalier ("Papa Doc") in April 1971.

Duvalier had appointed as successor his son, Jean Claude ("Baby Doc"), who lessened political oppression and sought to refurbish the international image of Haiti. U.S. aid programs were resumed, and various international agencies increased their direct assistance. Foreign capital began to develop new industries (such as the manufacture of baseballs), and tourism boomed. Still, unemployment remained high, and poverty continued to be the norm for most Haitians. Demonstrations hit the country in late 1985 and early 1986. Duvalier unleashed the dreaded Tonton Macoutes—a private army of plain-clothes thugs and killers organized by his father—but they were unable to contain the upheaval. As a result, the United States arranged for Duvalier to flee the country for exile in France, so that a five-member civilian-military council could try to bring democratic government to the island. Coups and failures of reform, however, characterized the government of Haiti into the 1990s.

In the 1970s there developed the phenomenon of the boat people, beginning with the Mariel exodus from Cuba and followed by a constant stream of refugees from Haiti. These refugees set sail in small boats, rafts, and even innertubes. Unknown numbers were lost at sea, and the United States was faced with the major dilemma of what to do. The U.S. Coast Guard and the navy assumed rescue operations, and in 1980 some 17,000 Haitians and 125,000 Cubans arrived in Florida. Most of the Cubans who sailed from the port of Mariel were among the island's poorest, and many were black. Although Congress in 1966 had extended permanent-resident status to all Cubans fleeing their country (except for serious criminals), the U.S. Immigration and Naturalization Service (INS) took the position that the Cubans in the Mariel boatlift were excludable aliens. The Mariel refugees were held in detention camps and prisons for several months, but after screening 123,000 were released on "parole." This meant that they could stay but were still classified as excludable aliens. The Cuban-Haitian Adjustment Act of 1986 legalized the status of all Cubans and Haitians who had come in 1980, with the exception of those with serious criminal records.

The Reagan administration worked out an arrangement with the Haitian government for the interception and return of refugees. Some of the Cubans who came into the country had been released from prisons and mental hospitals—a population the United States segregated and kept in detention camps. The Cuban government refused to discuss the return of this group until 1984, when an agreement was reached providing for their gradual repatriation. Castro periodically suspended the agreement, and fewer than 1,000 have been returned to Cuba. In addition, the same agreement allowed 20,000 Cubans per year to emigrate to the United States.

The issue of illegal immigration flared up again in 1991, with deteriorating conditions in Cuba and Haiti. The U.S. interest section in Havana was swamped with applications for visas, having issued some 36,000 during the first eight months of the year. Other Cubans tried to make it across the shark-infested Florida Straits in just about anything that would float. By August 1991 about 1,400 had survived the trip. Once again the Coast Guard became a rescue service.

Another exodus of Haitians began in the fall of 1991, after the military overthrew Haiti's first elected president in three decades, Rev. Jean-Bertrand Aristide. The Bush administration began to repatriate some of those who were rescued, but in late November a federal judge ordered a temporary ban on this practice. An Appeals Court overturned the ban, the judge reimposed it, and the courts began a game of musical decrees. But the way was cleared for some Haitians to be returned. More than 700 were given the status of "political refugee" and allowed to remain in the United States.

In the meantime, navy and Coast Guard ships began to overflow with refugees. After some 7,000 Haitians had been picked out of the sea, the Defense Department, in desperation, sent a task force to set up a tent camp at Guantanamo Bay. The Haitians rioted after being sent to the camp.

The Haitian situation was complicated even more by the country's internal politics. Aristide had been expelled from the Roman Catholic Salesian order for political radicalism and was well known for his anti-American position. Despite this, the United States quickly recognized his election and offered increased economic aid. When the military ousted him, the United States imposed an economic embargo on the country—probably the most important factor in driving people out. The embargo forced the closing of the plants that assembled clothing, sporting goods, and electronic consumer goods. As a result, some 100,000 Haitians lost their jobs. The restricted fuel deliveries to the island also curtailed the efforts of relief agencies to distribute food. Some liberals in the United States called for military intervention to restore democracy and argued that people were fleeing an undemocratic regime. The ghost of Woodrow Wilson probably chortled over the words of his ideological descendents.

But the Haitian situation was not the clearest case of democracy versus authoritarianism. During his short administration President Aristide defied the Parliament, which was forced to adjourn when a mob of his followers surrounded the building, attacked two legislators, and wrecked the office of an opposition political party. Earlier, the president's supporters had burned Haiti's Roman Catholic cathedral, the Vatican embassy, and a Communion host factory.[39] They also murdered the founder of the Christian Democratic party (the Protestant minister Sylvio Claude) and at least 25 other critics of the Aristide regime. The former priest clearly showed that he was not too different from his more secular predecessors. The embargo proved a failure in removing the military government. Its only success was in increasing the misery level of ordinary Haitians. In February 1992 the United States decided to substantially relax the embargo despite protests by the OAS, which continued its efforts to effect the return of Aristide. With the substantial removal of the Soviet Union from the Caribbean, a U.S. administration could even support an anti-U.S. government.

During the fall of 1992 large numbers of Haitians set sail for the United States. When the Bush administration ordered the Coast Guard to return these people to Haiti, candidate Bill Clinton denounced the policy as inhumane. After Clinton's victory in November reports began to emanate from Haiti that a virtual armada of small boats was being constructed in anticipation of the day when the new administration would receive the Haitian migrants with open arms. The president's advisers warned him that tens of thousands of Haitians pouring ashore at Palm Beach and Ft. Lauderdale would be a disaster for his administration, and Clinton quickly reinstated the Bush policy.

Clinton, however, did tighten the embargo and included oil in the list of proscribed goods. In June 1993 the Haitian military commander, General Raoul Cedras, agreed to meet with the exiled President Aristide to discuss the latter's return to office. Early in July a U.N.-mediated agreement was hammered out in New York. After first rejecting it, Aristide finally decided to accept. Among other things the agreement provided that: (a) Aristide would nominate a new prime minister who would then be confirmed by the Haitian Parliament, (b) Parliament would enact an amnesty law for the soldiers who had overthrown Aristide, (c) the military high command and police chief would resign, (d) a new military command would be appointed, (e) an international advisory group of some 1,600 soldiers and police from France, Canada, and the United States would go to Haiti to form an independent police force and retrain the army, and (f) Aristide would resume the presidency on 30 October 1993.

The plan seemed to be working as a new prime minister, Robert Malval, was installed and a new cabinet was appointed. An army-backed group called the Front for the Advancement and Progress of Haiti demanded a role in the new administration. Malval rejected this demand. Then in September mobs of anti-Aristide Haitians, supported by the police and army, began to roam the streets cracking whips, making voodoo signs, waving the black and red flag of the late "Papa Doc" Duvalier, and chanting, "Give us back our country."[40] Several pro-Aristide Haitians, including the new justice minister, were killed during the next few weeks, and most of the cabinet went into hiding.

A crisis developed when the USS *Harlan County* approached the coast of Haiti in mid-October with some 200 U.S. troops, the first contingent of a planned force of 600 military trainers and engineers. A mob of yelling Haitians forced U.S. Embassy personnel to leave the dock area, and the decision was made not to try to land the U.S. forces. Then, on 15 October, President Clinton sent six warships into Haitian waters to enforce his renewed oil embargo and dispatched a reinforced Marine rifle company to Guantanamo Bay, Cuba. State Department officials also announced that ships from France, Canada, and Argentina would join the naval cordon, and one such official stated, "We want these people to realize that we are willing to back up our words with force."[41]

Thus in mid-October Bill Clinton seemed ready to emulate Woodrow Wilson and employ American military forces to uplift and democratize the Caribbean. Walter Hines Paige had likened Wilson's policy to "shooting people into self-government." The Clinton administration has not yet selected a slogan. Perhaps if one were to visit the cemeteries at such Marine bases as Quantico or Paris Island on a quiet night, one could, with a good spiritual ear, hear far-off voices of departed leathernecks from the old corps singing that ballad from the 1916 intervention:

Damn, damn, damn the Haitian cacos
Button-scarred, voodoo-dancing drones,
Underneath the broiling sun,
Let them have the Benet-gun
And return us to our beloved homes.[42]

To an extent the question of Puerto Rican status subsided after 1952. The *independistas* set off some bombs within the United States during the 1960s and 1970s, but most Puerto Ricans repudiated such terrorist action. The island's economy grew, and by 1964 manufacturing accounted for 23 percent of the island's income. Between 1940 and 1964 the GNP increased nearly nine-fold and manufacturing output went up 18 times. By 1960 Puerto Rico had a higher ratio of cars to people than any other country in the world except the mainland United States. By 1988 the per capita income had risen to $5,157—less than half that of the state of Mississippi but still the highest in Latin America.

To spur economic development on the island, Congress enacted Section 936 of the Internal Revenue Code, which exempts Puerto Rican operations of U.S. companies from federal taxes. Some 300 companies have taken advantage of Section 936 and other tax breaks. Some 80 percent of all industrial jobs stem from these tax breaks, and Puerto Rico has become the world's largest producer of pharmaceuticals, with such companies as Eli Lilly, Pfizer, and Wang Laboratories. Eighty percent of the tuna consumed in the U.S. is processed in two Puerto Rican plants and carry such labels as Starkist and Bumblebee. Some Puerto Rican companies have begun to incorporate in the United States in order to take advantage of Section 936. Additional tax reforms in 1976 were aimed at attracting European capital, and by some estimates approximately $8 billion have been deposited in San Juan banks.

In August 1989 Puerto Rico adopted legislation designed to promote international banking on the island. The legislation offers a number of incentives to foreign and U.S. banks, such as complete tax exemption and a broad range of powers. Banks are able to operate in leasing, insurance, and securities, as well as traditional banking enterprises. Also, they are exempt from U.S. banking regulation. Owing to the island's status, companies opening international banking entities in Puerto Rico will have access to the U.S. market without burden of taxation. Through this legislation, Puerto Rico hopes to become more competitive with the Cayman Islands or the Bahamas in regard to banking.

The Communist bloc, led by Cuba, has been trying since the 1960s to have the United Nations put Puerto Rico back on its list of colonies (it was removed in 1953). On an annual basis the Cubans and the Puerto Rican *independistas* have brought the issue to the U.N. Decolonization Committee and received support from the so-called nonaligned nations. In 1973 they achieved some results when the committee recognized Puerto Rico's "inalienable right to self-determination and independence." The committee also recommended that no measures be taken but that the matter should be kept under review. The committee did continue its attack on the United States, and in November 1982 it recommended that the case of Puerto Rico be put on the agenda of the U.N. General Assembly. The Reagan administration struck back, and in a parliamentary maneuver it was established that there would not be a vote on Puerto Rican status.[43] Still, the ritual of holding hearings and attacking the United States would continue year after year, even though the United States has clearly stated its position that the committee has no authority in the matter of Puerto Rico.

In 1972 Governor Rafael Hernández Colón began an effort to replace the Federal Relations Act. An ad hoc committee was formed with seven Puerto Rican members and seven from the United States. The Puerto Rican members prepared a draft proposal, the U.S. members reviewed these, and the full committee issued a revised draft. This proposal stipulated that the phrase "Free Associated State" be substituted for commonwealth and made other changes in the authority of both governments. The Compact for Permanent Union was introduced into the House of Representatives in late 1975 and died in committee.

In December 1976 President Gerald Ford announced that he would ask Congress to grant statehood to Puerto Rico. This bolt from the blue surprised everyone, and Ford later explained that he did it because "it was the right thing to do."[44] The bill was introduced in January 1977 but was buried, owing in part to Puerto Rican opposition. The Carter administration discussed the situation and issued a proclamation on self-determination.

During the 1980 presidential campaign, Ronald Reagan promised to introduce statehood legislation, but as president he did not get beyond making the ritual statement concerning the principle of self-determination. The statehood group in Puerto Rico felt betrayed and reacted angrily, to no avail. Vice President George Bush took up their cause and owing in part to his urging, Kansas Senator Robert Dole and Representative Robert J. Lagomassino of California introduced bills that would provide for a referendum. In 1988 the Republican party platform reiterated the party's support for statehood, while the Democrats came out for commonwealth.

In a surprise move, the Democratic Governor of Puerto Rico, Hernández Colón, called for a status plebiscite. Newly elected President Bush called for the same thing in his 1989 State of the Union address and reiterated his own support for statehood. The Senate Energy Committee under the leadership of Senator Bennett Johnston of Louisiana set to work on a bill that would outline the choices to be decided in a referendum. The committee insisted on spelling out the specific details of each choice, so that the Puerto Ricans would know precisely what they were voting for. And the Congress would then agree to completely accept the results.

This proved to be a stumbling block. Governor Hernández Colón submitted the "enhanced Commonwealth" proposals that he had prepared several years before. In effect, these would give Puerto Rico most of the advantages of independence while retaining most of the privileges of statehood. For example, one proposal would give the governor of Puerto Rico the power to declare federal laws inapplicable on the island. As a matter of fact, Governor Hernández Colón had tried to implement some of these on his own and had been rebuked by the State Department for negotiating a tax-sparing agreement with Japan in 1985. The Senate committee did not accept the governor's proposals.

In September 1989 the Senate committee approved a bill by a vote of 11 to 8. This provided some transition steps in the event of a vote either for independence or statehood. A storm of debate erupted in both Puerto Rico and the United States and raged throughout 1990 and 1991. In Puerto Rico a heated argument focused on what the island would gain or lose. The Statehood and Independence parties charged that commonwealth status was really colonialism, while the Commonwealth party replied that either of the other two choices would lead to economic suicide. Some observers believed that the whole issue was becoming a referendum on Section 936 of the tax code. One of the few clear results has been equal billing for the Independence party, which received $500,000 in federal funds for the referendum campaign. Ironically, most of the *independenistas* live in the United States.[45]

In the United States some groups argue that Puerto Rico will be given preferential treatment if the people elect statehood. Some unions have launched an effort to modify or repeal Section 936, charging that it encourages companies to "run away" to Puerto Rico. For instance, American Home Products (AHP) manufactures aspirin in its Elkhart, Indiana, Whitehall Laboratories. AHP shifted some of its product lines to a new Puerto Rican plant and announced the closing of Whitehall Laboratories in late 1990. The Chemical Workers union charges that at least 21 companies enjoying 936 status are "runaways" and it is suing AHP. In Congress, Representative Pete Stark has introduced a bill to deny 936 tax breaks to such businesses. If the bill passes, it could add another argument for the Statehood party.[46]

In October 1990 the House passed a bill providing for a plebescite. The Senate version was so different, however, that reconciliation efforts failed, and the bills died when Congress adjourned.

As the issue dragged out into 1991, Governor Hernández Colón tried to force the issue by asking for a referendum on whether or not there should be a referendum on the status issue. The Puerto Rican legislature rejected his proposal but referred another bill to voters that would be nonbinding but symbolic. On 8 December 1991 Puerto Rican voters rejected a bill that asserted the island's "right to freedom" from U.S. subordination and to its "cultural distinctiveness." The bill was supported by both pro-commonwealth and pro-independence groups.

On 3 November 1992 the voters of Puerto Rico gave an overwhelming vote to the New Progressive party, which champions statehood. The NPP captured the governorship, control of both houses of the legislature, most municipal offices, and the island's nonvoting member of Congress. The Popular Democratic party (the Commonwealth status party) suffered its worst defeat in 54 years, even though its candidate for governor was the daughter of Luis Muñoz Marin. The new governor, Pedro Rossello, promised a referendum on the status issue at an early date.

In mid-1993 the Puerto Rican legislature passed legislation making both English and Spanish the official languages (Spanish had been the only official language) and authorizing a plebiscite on the status issue. Although nonbinding on the United States, the statehood proposal contains a mandate demanding Puerto Rico's admission to the union. Several U.S. senators have pledged to introduce such legislation if the statehood proposal wins. Because Puerto Rico votes heavily Democratic, a Democratic-controlled U.S. Congress would probably jump at the chance to secure another solidly Democratic state.

The statehood element was given some urgency when Clinton's budget cutters went after the Section 936 exemption during the 1993 budget planning. A lobbying blitz salvaged most of the tax break, but Puerto Ricans saw this as proof that their status was under siege. In addition, the proposed North

American Free Trade Agreement (NAFTA) seemed to threaten the possible diversion of U.S. investments to Mexico.

On 14 November 1993 Puerto Ricans went to the polls and voted for commonwealth status: the commonwealth option received 48.4 percent of the vote and the statehood option 46.2 percent; the option for independence came in at 4 percent.

President Reagan's Caribbean Basin Initiative (CBI) called for three main developments: (a) a 12-year period of duty-free entry into the United States for all Caribbean products except textiles and apparel; (b) tax incentives for U.S. businesses that invest in new plants in CBI countries; and (c) an emergency supplemental foreign aid appropriation for currency support operations. Congress quickly approved the last initiative, which was implemented in September. The other two measures died with the end of the 97th Congress.

Reintroduced in the next session, the other two measures underwent considerable modification at the hands of Congress. The tax-incentive plan was eliminated and replaced by a provision allowing U.S. businesses to take income tax deductions for expenses incurred while attending conventions in CBI countries. The number of items excluded from the duty-free list was increased to include footwear, handbags, luggage, work gloves, canned tuna, and petroleum and petroleum products. An important product, sugar, was already on the duty-free list, but imports had been tightly controlled since the sugar marketing system had been devised in the 1930s.

In 1986 the Reagan administration bypassed the congressional roadblock and created two important programs. The first provided for guaranteed access levels for U.S. imports of textile products assembled in CBI countries from fabric cut and formed in the United States. Section 807a was labeled "super 807." The second was part of the tax reform measure completed in late 1986. According to a government source, "This authorized the use of U.S. Tax Code Section 936 funding from Puerto Rico for investment in eligible CBI countries. Under 936 funding, the large amount of funds generated by U.S. investors in Puerto Rico can be re-lent at below market rates to finance twin plant operations, various other investments, and development projects in CBI beneficiaries."[47] To qualify for 936 loans countries must sign a Tax Information Exchange Agreement (TIEA) with the United States. Several projects have been funded in this manner, including a cardboard box manufacturing company in Dominica, projects for Air Jamaica, and the Jamaica leg of a submarine fiber-optic communications network by AT&T.

Some critics have charged that trade actually declined after 1983—some 25 percent by 1987. The drop in value of petroleum exports, however, more than accounts for all this decline. Nonpetroleum exports from CBI countries increased 23 percent, and exports of nontraditional products (usually manufactured goods) grew by more than 50 percent. In the 12-month period ending in June 1989, nontraditional exports totaled $3.4 billion, representing an increase of more than 88 percent since 1983. While foreign aid substantially declined in the late 1980s, industrial development in the CBI definitely increased. The Dominican Republic and Jamaica have established free-trade zones, and companies such as Westinghouse, Baxter Travenol, and Hanes have built plants in the former country. Electronic assembly industries have been constructed in the Dominican Republic, Jamaica, and St. Christopher-Nevis.

The value of horticultural products exported to the United States increased 45 percent between 1983 and 1988. Some of the most significant gains were fresh pineapples, frozen concentrated orange juice, cantaloupes, melons, lemons, mangoes, and frozen broccoli.

A major breakthrough came in August 1990 when President Bush signed legislation making the CBI permanent. The original plan had been to push for another 12-year program, but the permanency element added real stability to the CBI. The measure, however, continued the exclusions of the first plan. The CBI has obviously not met all the expectations raised in 1982. But the Reagan-Bush free-trade push has had positive results. President Joaquin Balaguer of the Dominican Republic called the CBI "the most constructive initiative which has ever come to Latin America . . . a pragmatic movement which has achieved a great deal of practical good. . . . The Dominican Republic specifically has improved its economy, has progressed, has established a large number of free trade zones drawing industries for export, and thus has reduced its unemployment rate a great deal."[48]

The United States has played an important economic and political role in the Caribbean. Except for Cuba, most of this impact has come in the twentieth century. Outside of Cuba, the U.S. Virgin Islands, and Puerto Rico, the role of the United States only became significant during and after World War II.

The economic impact is not only acknowledged but even vastly exaggerated by those who are most hostile to United States' presence in the region. "Dependency theorists" argue that the United States has forced nations of the Caribbean and elsewhere to fall into a state of total dependency on the United States. This is called "neo-imperialism" to distinguish it from what this writer would call authentic imperialism, which can be documented.

At one time the words *empire* and *imperialism* had specific meaning and content. *The Oxford Universal Dictionary* defines the former as "supreme and extensive political dominion" and "absolute sway, supreme control." Imperialism is the process of creating empires, and colonies were the logical result. With the collapse of colonialism after World War II, neo-Leninists found it necessary to redefine imperialism so as to continue to denounce any role a capitalistic power might play in the world. Because "supreme dominion" had disappeared, they had to create a theoretical system and mythology of "informal" or "hidden" imperialism. Thus economic ties (translated by neo-Leninists as "control") became the key to "neo-imperialistic" theory, and *dependency* became the official buzzword. P. T. Bauer of the London School of Economics writes of this phenomenon, "The terms economic colonialism and neo-colonialism have sprung up recently to describe almost any form of economic relation between relatively rich and poor countries, regions, or groups. This terminology confuses poverty with colonial status, a concept which has always been understood to mean lack of political sovereignty. Since the late 1960's, the usage has been extended to cover the activities of multinational corporations in the Third World. . . . Thus not only does the new terminology reflect a debasement of language; it also distorts the truth."[49]

In the real world all economies (except purely subsistence ones) are dependent on others for something. In the case of the United States one can point to petroleum, tin, and a host of other minerals, in addition to markets. Cuba provides an excellent test case for this theory. As Cuba sees it, after 1899 the United States forced Cuba to grow two crops for export—sugar and tobacco. Thus Cuba was locked in the iron grip of the "Colossus of the North" long after the last U.S. troops left the island. Cuba's Communist government argues that after 1959 Fidel Castro liberated the country from this dependency web and brought about true independence. Conditions in Cuba in 1993 do not, however, sustain this argument. Over 30 years after Castro's ascent to power Cuba is more dependent than ever on the export of sugar and is heavily dependent on subsidies from the Soviet Union. Thousands of young Cubans have been killed and wounded fighting as proxies in foreign wars. The island cannot produce enough basic foodstuffs to feed the population, and Cubans are being forced back to the country to live the lives of subsistence farmers. So much for the dependency theory. Soil, climate, and culture have more to do with economic development than outside factors.

The United States continues to play an important role in the economy of the Caribbean, except for Cuba. The United States buys the products of the area and sends goods, capital, and technology. U.S. tourists pour a considerable amount of money into the coffers of the islands, and this is an industry that has boomed since the 1950s. Many Caribbean islands now sport highrise hotels and casinos to lure the yankee dollar. In part, this reflects the relative freedom of travel in the region. A tourist rarely needs a visa, and travelers can enter and leave countries with few complications. In fact, it is more complicated to reenter the United States than it is to enter most Caribbean countries—again, Cuba excepted.

The political role of the United States has been rather ambiguous. It has been quite important in both Cuba and Puerto Rico, as the United States ousted the old empire of Spain and incorporated both in a new imperial relationship. Certainly some of the xenophobia of Cuban nationalism can be attributed to a reaction against the presence of the United States—even if part of this was mythical. At times the U.S. ideals of independence, democracy, and free elections have had some impact on some countries. How extensive this has been can be argued ad infinitum. Puerto Rico, the Dominican Republic, and Grenada are all more democratic than they were 50 or 100 years ago. But what about Haiti? The poor island is the same in 1991 as it was in 1810 or 1915. Again, culture, geography, and history are probably more important than U.S. influence.

chapter 5

THE UNITED STATES AND THE CARIBBEAN'S CAULDRON OF CULTURES

The interaction between the predominantly Anglo-European United States and the multiethnic Caribbean world has produced some interesting developments. This area of cultural influence has often been controversial, especially when the subject is the United States' impact on the peoples and cultures of the Caribbean. When the historian Daniel Boorstin described Puerto Rican culture as "American with vague vestiges of the Spanish past," René Marquis charged that Boorstin's opinion was that of a "beardless intellectual" who had only visited the island for three weeks.[1]

Usually the intellectual-academic-writer types are most critical of the United States' cultural influence on the Caribbean, as has been the case for the last hundred years or more. These groups believe in a kind of cultural Garden of Eden before the yankee serpent corrupted the inhabitants and bemoan or curse the insidious influence of the Colossus. "Coca-Colonization" is one phrase used to convey this message, as is the Disney character Donald Duck as an instrument of social oppression. Ironically, many of those who sport this view display the trappings of the so-called oppresser. When Daniel Ortega campaigned for president he wore blue jeans, cowboy boots, and played rock music at his rallies. Fidel Castro is quite addicted to blonde Nordic-looking women and luxury cars (not Russian made). Even when trying to look militant and anti-American, all commandantes wear U.S. Army fatigues. Interestingly, the foreign minister of Nicaragua until 1990 was Rev. Miguel d'Escoto, a Maryknoll priest. During the salad days of power he drove a Mercedes and sported hand-tailored safari suits (à la Ernest Hemingway).

It is obvious that most who claim to hate U.S. culture in reality hate democracy and the common people. The historian Frederick Pike has noted, "Early in the twentieth century, the Latin American ruling elite had begun to utilize the presence of United States capital in their quest to preserve a traditional society and to avoid what they perceived as the revolutionary consequences of penetration by United States political culture. . . . [T]hey were hostile to the Colossus of the North not so much because they feared its political imperialism . . . as because they feared that penetration of its cultural values would herald social revolution."[2] This is as true for the elite of the Communist left in Cuba and Nicaragua as it is for the traditional right wing. Both want to preserve a two-tier society and see the pop culture of the United States as having deep political implications.

A recent observer of the revolutionary impact of this culture wrote, "The spread of American products is in large part the spread of American culture. Blue jeans are not bought out of some universal denim aesthetic. Nor is the appeal of Pepsi and Coke rooted in some universal taste. Buying the products is a way to share in the American dream: Conspicuous consumption is a way of joining American consumer culture." The author noted that people are buying into the American dream:

> Those dreams are about individual freedom, the freedom of people to create themselves anew, redefining themselves through the products they buy, the clothes they wear and the music they listen to. . . . That social freedom is intimately tied to American politics, which celebrates individual power and [provides] the chance for the common man to play the political game. The appeal of the American ideal flows from its popular source. American culture is popular abroad largely because it is popular culture: it is by and for the masses rather than social elites.[3]

McDonald's Hamburguesa or KFC's Pollo Frito are hated as much by the left as by the right because they imply individual choice for the masses. Rev. Ernesto Cardenal, the Roman Catholic priest who served as Nicaraguan minister of culture, once wrote that Havana under Castro was a "city that is bound to please a monk" because in essence the people were forced to live like monks in poverty with no private property.[4]

The Cuban exile writer and playwright Carlos Alberto Montaner has observed that "for two centuries the United States has been part and parcel of Cuba's national environment." After listing a number of consequences of that relationship he states, "Practically all the key elements that comprised the habitat of Cuba's national being were in one way or another related to the geographic accident of the island's close proximity to a huge, powerful, trade-oriented and creative nation. . . .The United States gave shape, content, and direction to the fragile and dependent society that dwelled in a small island 90 miles from its shores." He concludes, "Considering the poverty, ignorance, history, and cultural features of Cuban society, it could not have been otherwise. Cuba was a country geared for imitation, not for spontaneous creation." And he advises Cubans (and other countries in the Caribbean) to banish "adversary nationalism" and to adopt a "partisan nationalism" that "identifies and underscores the traits common to Cuba and the United States to the degree that the latter is the core of world civilization, and the former is one if its closest cultural appendices." When it comes to antibiotics, computers, or supersonic travel, "we are all Yankees."[5]

The Caribbean influence on the United States has been less dramatic and more subtle. The Caribbean has added spices to the melting pot of American culture without significantly modifying the flavor. Caribbean products such as sugar, bananas, mangoes, rum, and cigars have added to the quality of life without constituting essential goods. And many residents of the United States dance the limbo, listen to calypso music, drink daiquiris and piña colladas, smoke Macanudo cigars, and vacation in the Caribbean. In all probability most of this Caribbean influence has been transmitted through American travelers, as Caribbean immigrants have tended to live in closely knit ethnic neighborhoods. One could almost call them more insulated from the broader culture than other immigrant groups. For example, Mexican restaurants are found in various parts of many towns and cities and cater to a broad clientele. How many Cuban or Jamaican restaurants can one find outside of those neighborhoods?

Some Caribbean influence on American music appeared in the 1830s and 1840s in New Orleans. Louis Moreau Gottschalk, who is considered the first true, classically trained American composer, blended traditional European style music with that of the black slaves and Creoles. He traveled and performed in the Caribbean and composed pieces with various musical elements from the region. In 1859 on the island of Guadeloupe he composed the symphony *A Night in the Tropics*, which a critic has described as "a North American paying his respects to Latin American music much in the spirit with which a succession of French composers . . . would express their kinship to Spanish music." This unique symphony ends with an explosion of melodies "some foreshadowing the modern 'samba.'"[6] Gottschalk also—whose music influenced Bizet, Borodin, and Debussy—used Caribbean dance music in his *Souvenir de Porto Rico—Marche des Gibaros* and *Ojos Criollos—Danse Cubaine*. The latter blends American cakewalk music with the habanera.

Twentieth-century Caribbean music has been incorporated into various aspects of American popular music. In the early 1960s Mongo Santamaria, a Cuban musician living in the United States, combined cha-cha, guapacha, and rock and roll in what he called "cha-cha rock." In New Orleans Henry Roland Byrd, known as "Professor Longhair," mixed Caribbean music with blues, boogie-woogie, and big band music in his own unique way. This great jazz pianist, from whom Elvis Presley "borrowed" in copious amounts, said, "I used to take all these things and put 'em in one big bag and shake 'em up and make a gumbo out of 'em."[7] One of his classic pieces, "Tipitina," is a vivid example of a musical gumbo with Caribbean spices.

Some contemporary rock groups have also made use of Jamaican reggae. The reciprocal nature of musical relationships can be seen in the "Rude Boy" music that came out of the slums of Kingston, Jamaica, in the mid-1960s. The Motown sound of James Brown was the basis of this style. Puerto Ricans such as Tito Puente, Noro Morales, and José Feliciano have combined Caribbean music with soul and rock.

One of the best examples of the kind of symbiotic relationship between the United States and the Caribbean can be found in the sport of baseball. Cuban Creoles who came to the United States in the nineteenth century as students, tourists, or businessmen brought the sport to Cuba. By the 1870s the sport was spreading rapidly, and in 1878 the Cuban League of Professional Baseball was organized. It was the second professional baseball league in the Western Hemisphere. Cubans were rejecting the Spanish sport of bullfighting for what was becoming the American national pastime.[8]

Cuba also became the place where some American major league teams spent the winter honing their skills playing Cuban teams. And black players from the U.S. Negro League came to Cuba to play on the Cuban teams against the white players they were not allowed to face in the States. During the 1910 winter season Ty Cobb of the Detroit Tigers placed fourth in batting with a record of .385. He was surpassed by John Henry Lloyd (.500), Grant "Home Run" Jackson (.412) and Bruce Petaway (.390), all from the Negro League. Interestingly, about half the money used to make the New York Yankees "the best team that money can buy," came from Cuba. Colonel Tillinghast L'Hommedieu Huston served in Cuba during the Spanish-American War and remained to make a considerable fortune in construction projects. In 1915, in partnership with the beer baron Jacob Ruppert, he purchased the Yankees. Later they bought the services of "Babe" Ruth, and built Yankee Stadium.

Cubans carried baseball to other Caribbean countries, but baseball players of color were not accepted in the United States until after Jackie Robinson broke the color barrier in 1947; subsequently major league teams began to look to Cuba for talent. In 1960 so many Cubans were playing for the Washington Senators that they had the major league's only all-Cuban triple play: Pedro Ramos to Julio Becquer to José Valdivielso. In fact, a young Fidel Castro tried out for the Washington Senators but was rejected. Some believe that if he had gotten a major league contract there might not have been a revolution in Cuba. Not long after the triumph of Fidel Castro this flow of players stopped, except for an occasional player who would escape. Luis Tiant and José Canseco, for example, became stars in the U.S. after getting out of Cuba. After the 1992 season Tony Perez was named manager of the Cincinnati Reds. He was the first Cuban (or Caribbean native) to reach this level in the sport.

The major leagues still look at Cuba with hopeful eyes as baseball continues to be the national sport of the island and Cuban teams regularly win in international, amateur competitions. And, the major leagues still beckon to Cuban players. In August 1991 René Arocha of the Cuban national team defected after his team competed in the United States. His wife said, "He thought that if he lived in a capitalist country he could play in the Major League. He always dreamed of playing there."[9] Ironically, a 1977 edict by the commissioner of baseball prohibits Cuban nationals from signing contracts with U.S. major league teams. Still, with the vast changes going on, many in baseball expect Cubans to be playing on U.S. teams, and one former manager stated that within 10 years as many as 20 Cuban players would be on U.S. teams.[10]

Players also began to come to the U.S. from Puerto Rico and the Dominican Republic. Stars such as Roberto Clemente, Orlando Cepeda, and Vic Power came from Puerto Rico. The Chicago Cubs have had the most effective scouting effort there, and Luis Rosa has some 18 players who have made it in the major leagues. These include Benito Santiago, Sandy Alomar, Jr., Roberto Alomar, and Ivan Calderon. By 1991, 20 professional baseball organizations ran camps or acadamies in the Dominican Republic. One of these was Japanese, the Hiroshima Toyo Carp. The most successful have been those of the Los Angeles Dodgers and the Toronto Blue Jays. In fact, in 1990 more Dominican than U.S. high school graduates signed their first baseball contract. The island has produced such stars as Juan Marichall, the Alou brothers (Felipe, Jesus, and Mateo), Julian Javier, and Manny Mota. By the 1990s Venezuela was also becoming an important source of major league talent. The 1992 World Series (Toronto Blue Jays versus the Atlanta Braves) had eight players from the Caribbean region—three from Puerto Rico and five from the Dominican Republic.[11]

Immigration from the Caribbean to the United States began in the latter half of the nineteenth century. More than 100,000 Cubans left the island, and most came to the United States. They settled in cities along the eastern seaboard, but most stayed in Key West and Tampa, Florida. The cigar-making industry boomed as Cubans brought their skills north to create new factories. By 1900 the cigar industry in Tampa was worth some $17 million. Puerto Rican immigration began in the twentieth century, but the major influx of people from the Caribbean began after World War II. This was especially the case during the 1960s, 1970s, and 1980s.

Prior to 1900 relatively few people from the British West Indies migrated to America. During the first decade of the twentieth century about 30,000 emigrated, and this increased to 60,000 during the next decade. Until Congress slammed the door on West Indian immigration on 1 July 1924, some 40,000 more West Indians arrived. A large number of these settled in New York City, especially in Harlem. They tended to be high-church Anglicans, with a strong work ethic and a devotion to education. By 1969 the incomes of West Indians in New York City were 28 percent higher than the incomes of other New York blacks and 52 percent higher than black incomes nationwide. Even by the 1920s American blacks were calling the West Indians "black Jews."[12]

The list of distinguished blacks of West Indian origin is impressive. Barbara Watson was the first woman to be named an assistant secretary of state. Her father, James Watson, started as an elevator operator and became the first black judge in New York City. Richard Lopez was one of America's first aerospace engineers. J. Bruce Llewellyn is one of the richest black men in the United States. And four-star general Colin Powell (whose parents came from Jamaica in the early 1920s) served as chairman of the Joint Chiefs of Staff (the highest military position in the nation) from 1989 until his retirement in September 1993.

Thousands of immigrants, both legal and illegal, streamed north from Puerto Rico, the Dominican Republic, Jamaica, Haiti, Cuba, and Central America. By 1980 more than two million Puerto Ricans lived in the United States. Forty-nine percent lived in New York State, as opposed to 64 percent in 1970. Approximately 800,000 Cubans had immigrated to the United States by 1980, and 59 percent of these lived in Florida. To date, assimilation has been slow, and enclaves of Haitians, Dominicans, Jamaicans, and others can be found in several large cities.

Cubans have had a profound impact on south Florida. They transformed the economy of the Miami area from one based on tourism and retirees to a bustling, diversified mixture of banks, industries (such as food processing), and retail stores. Capital poured into "Little Havana" from Latin America, and by 1978 Miami ranked second to New York in the number of banks specializing in international banking. More than nine companies doing business with Latin America had headquarters in the city. Miami's annual Trade Fair of the Americas generates millions of dollars in income, as does international commerce (estimated at some $4 billion in 1982). Cuban residents also renovated much of the inner-city slums of Miami, and their savings-bank assets have skyrocketed.

Unlike Puerto Rican or other Caribbean immigrants, most Cubans have become strong supporters of the Republican party. Initially, many exiles registered as Democrats but left the party during the Carter administration because they believed it was soft on communism. They view the United States as a refuge from Communist tyranny and have generally supported the foreign policies of Reagan and Bush. A good example of these developments is Jorge Mas Canosa, who founded the influential Cuban American National Foundation after making his fortune in construction. Mas was a member of Brigade 2506, which landed at the Bay of Pigs. After being freed, he worked as a shoe salesman, milkman, and construction worker. Eventually he owned the company. He and his foundation played a key role in building congressional support for Radio Marti and TV Marti. In 1985 he persuaded Florida Senator Claude Pepper to cosponsor legislation to repeal the 1976 Clark Amendment, which had prohibited all U.S. funding of the anti-Communist insurgents in Angola. The repeal effort was successful.

Mas hopes someday to return to a free Cuba, but many in the second generation are content with being Americans. Some still join Alpha-66 and train in the woods of south Florida, but most are not as angry as their parents. The "yucas," as they are called (young, upwardly mobile Cuban Americans) are bilingual and bicultural. A recent poll found that 60 percent of those under age 34 would not return to Cuba under any circumstances.[13]

The energy and success of the Cubans has aroused some anger and hostility among other groups. There have been some violent clashes between Cubans, blacks, and Haitians. The latter two groups mistakenly assume that Cuban immigrants have received massive government handouts. The limited amount of refugee assistance extended by the U.S. government has been much less per capita than aid received by Puerto Ricans in New York. The politics of jealousy is one of the basic elements of human society. One Cuban stated humorously and succinctly, "We came too fast, too many were successful. Some of us are too arrogant, too loud—and play dominoes till 2 in the morning."[14]

The influx of Caribbean immigrants has had some unpleasant consequences for the United States. As the cocaine trade developed in Colombia, the Caribbean became a main trade route and trans-shipment center for U.S.-bound drugs. By the early 1980s most of the cocaine headed for the United States was being trans-shipped through the Bahamas. Increasingly, the shipments consisted of a different sort of drug—a crack-cocaine prototype called "rock." According to some authorities, rock was developed in the Netherlands Antilles through a process of converting coca paste with soda, water, and rum. The process moved through the Caribbean to the United States, and a variety of gangs began to push the more potent form of cocaine.

A Dominican gang opened up the New York City market for crack in the mid-1980s. Well organized, the gang delivered high-quality crack in vials marked "Based Balls." The Colombians preferred doing business with Dominicans rather than with Americans because of their common language and earlier deals involving marijuana. The Colombian gangs extended operations from their New York City base to Providence, Rhode Island; Stamford, Connecticut; and other New England cities.

Jamaican gangs began to play an important, and murderous, role in the crack trade and in gun running. Traveling Jamaican gangs called "posses" moved out of Florida into various cities. By mid-1991 some authorities estimated that some 40 posses, with 22,000 members, were in operation, controlling about one-third of the crack trade. The posses are well known for their their reckless violence. The Shower posse carries that title because in firefights with other gangs it showers an area with bullets. Since 1985 the Bureau of Alcohol, Tobacco, and Firearms has documented more than 3,000 posse-related homocides in the United States. Jamaican posses have been active in such cities as Dallas, Texas, and Kansas City, Missouri. The majority of Caribbean immigrants are honest people who want to improve their economic condition in lawful ways. Of course you know this if the man who takes care of your yard, plants flowers in your flower boxes, owns an impressive stock portfolio, voted for Ronald Reagan, and is building a library in his hometown, is a native of Jamaica.[15]

For a number of years gambling has provided another link between the United States and the Caribbean. Until 1960 Cuba was the main locus of casino gambling, and the organized crime syndicate in America ran a lush operation under the direction of Meyer Lansky. When Castro brought dictatorship and "holiness" to the island, casino gambling spread to various other locales. In early 1992 an interesting development came to light when authorities in the Dominican Republic, with U.S. assistance, broke up the largest gambling operation in U.S. history. The mob-controlled sports-gambling system had been moved to the Dominican Republic and was operating with satellite dishes. This $100 million-per-month operation had a series of 800 telephone numbers by which bettors on the mainland could place their wagers on all kinds of sports. The telephones were still ringing madly as Dominican police shut down the operation.

Any generalization about the interaction between the cultures of the United States and the Caribbean world runs head on into the diverse and complex ethnic and cultural mixture of the latter. Even people from the same island are sometimes different and react in dissimilar ways to the United States. For example, the Lopez-Watson-Llewellyn-Powell clan came from Jamaica, fit right in with American culture, and excelled in various fields. Marcus Garvey also came from Jamaica, but he rejected American culture and founded the United Negro Improvement Association, an organization advocating black separatism and the "back to Africa" campaign. The Rastafarian immigrant from Jamaica with his dreadlocks is as different from General Colin Powell's high-church Anglican father as rum is from scotch. And the cultural interaction is completely different.

In much the same way, rum and Coca-Cola can differ according to the type of rum. The light rum of Bacardí makes a most palatable Cuba Libre (another name for this traditional drink that says something for the time and circumstance of the mixture), but the dark and heavy Appleton rum from the J. Wray & Nephew distillery in Jamaica produces a drink resembling old-fashioned cough medicine. Cultural contacts and mixtures follow a similar pattern. Some cultural elements blend and harmonize—others clash.

In a recent book about baseball in the Dominican Republic, one of the persons interviewed noted that during the 1920s the people of that country were fans "of the unlikely combination of Augusto Cesar Sandino and the New York Yankees."[16] This peculiar mixture of conflicting heroes—the anti-Yankee guerrilla leader and the quintessential team of the American national pastime—is very typical of the historical mixture of rum and Coca-Cola.

CONCLUSION

The choices facing U.S. officials have rarely been easy ones—and certainly not clear-cut ones between good and evil. This is especially true in the nation's traditional sphere of influence, the Caribbean–Central American region. Whatever the United States has done, or failed to do, some groups have been outraged. The leaders of the United States have not had a conscious or planned drive for empire, formal or informal. There have been various, and conflicting, drives, some of which have had imperial overtones, either in scope or method. But any action, or inaction, by a powerful nation like the United States has an impact on its weaker neighbors. In writing about Cuba, Roger Fontaine has noted that "no small power ever had an easy time of living next to a powerful neighbor. No small power, however, has had an easier time of it than Cuba. If this seems too hard to accept, the Cuban leadership might ask the Czechs, the Latvians, the Mongolians, the Nepalese, or the Irish what their experience has been."[1]

To talk about U.S. officials wanting a liberal-capitalistic world order is only to state their very general hopes and ideals; it does not give a blueprint or lay plans for specific courses of action. Concepts of world order form a kind of ideological background but do not dominate all thought and action. Day-to-day policies have been prompted by a more confused set of influences. In addition, the terms *liberal-capitalistic* and *open world* have had different meanings to different officials. Perhaps the most precise one can be is to say that American culture and its value system is by its very nature liberal and capitalistic. U.S. officials have simply reflected their culture in various ways.

At times the United States has gone overboard with crusading zeal and idealistic pretentions. The Good Neighbor Policy and the Alliance for Progress created false expectations on all sides. U.S. leaders really believed that their country was loved and respected for the beauty of its soul, the strength of its character, and the value of its ideals. During the 1940s especially it seemed that the Good Neighbor declarations and actions, combined with the victory over the Axis powers, had given the United States' Latin American policy a plenary indulgence for all times. These attitudes produced a too glorified view of an inter-American system, which in reality had little effective substance, and the illusion of a democratic, middle-class Latin America that would naturally remain friendly with the United States because of assumed identity of interests and values. When the system faltered and illusions were challenged, U.S. leaders revived the practice of shoveling dollars, advisers, volunteers, and missions into Latin America. The Alliance for Progress even seemed to promise a Good Redeemer Policy. Well intended, although too paternalistic, these policies helped to stimulate the "revolution of rising expectations," the crisis of overpopulation, and angry denunciations about "dependency imperialism." In truth, there is little the United States can do to induce the peoples of the Caribbean and Latin America to love their northern neighbor. Discrepancies of wealth, power, and development will always promote other feelings—usually jealousy entwined with a desire to emulate. A prevailing and preponderant Latin American attitude about the United States can be illustrated by a story. Two women were vacationing at a Catskills resort and complaining about every aspect. One especially attacked the food, saying how terrible it was. The other nodded in vigorous agreement and added, "And the portions are so small." In other words, to some people, U.S. assistance and capital are terrible, but they would like to have more.

When all is said and done power politics remains one of the few constants in international affairs. The world is a messy, dangerous place and will remain so as long as people compete for power, resources, and all the other elements that emanate from human beings and their societies. The United States as a democratic-capitalistic nation can elect not to play the game, but it will bear the serious consequences of either default or loss, especially in its own back yard.

Certainly the United States has made its share of mistakes, has vacillated on too many occasions, has blundered in some circumstances, and has been too often plagued by self-doubt. Yet the significance of U.S. actions was clearly stated by the president of the Czech and Slovak Federal Republic, Vaclav Havel, in a speech to the North Atlantic Treaty Organization Council in March 1991: "The democratic west . . . succeeded in withstanding for years the expansion of a Communist-type totalitarian system, was for years offering sympathies to the democratic forces in the countries of the Soviet bloc and never ceased to believe that these forces would be victorious one day. . . . The protection of democracy and human liberty to which it has been committed has given encouragement and inspiration to citizens of our countries too. We have seen that a free society has so much respect for itself that it finds it worth the effort to protect itself against the menace of totalitarianism."[2]

Havel could have been speaking for the Caribbean–Central American area as much as for Eastern Europe. The Greek historian Thucydides wrote, "Men secure peace by using their power justly and by making it clear that they will not allow others to wrong them." The United States has not always followed these precepts in the Caribbean, but it has enough of the time, and the region is better off for it.

CHRONOLOGY

1741	British fleet fails to take St. Iago, Cuba.
1762	British take Havana, Cuba.
1763	British return Havana to Spain but take the Floridas.
1783	Spain closes Cuban ports to American ships; also closes the Mississippi River to American commerce.
1795	United States and Spain sign the Pinckney Treaty, which gives the former free navigation of the Mississippi River and the right of deposit at New Orleans for three years.
1798–1800	United States wages undeclared naval war with France in the Caribbean.
1803	United States purchases the Louisiana Territory from France and gains control of the mouth of the Mississippi River.
1819	Signing of Transcontinental Treaty with Spain gives the United States full possession of the Floridas.
1821	Caribbean squadron of the U.S. Navy established.
1846	Treaty of New Grenada signed.
1851	Clayton-Bulwer Treaty between United States and Great Britain concerning control of Central America is signed.

1850–1851	Narcisco Lopez twice attempts to take Cuba.
1854	Ostend Manifesto; *Black Warrior* crisis with Spain.
1867	U.S. Senate refuses to act on treaty to purchase the Danish Virgin Islands.
1870	Senate rejects treaty annexing the Dominican Republic.
1898	War with Spain; Treaty of Paris gives Puerto Rico to the United States, and Spain gives up Cuba; U.S. military government in Cuba established.
1900	Foraker Act gives Puerto Rico an elected House of Delegates.
1902	United States ends military government of Cuba and evacuates the island.
1902–1903	Venezuelan Crisis; U.S. fleet mobilizes off the coast of Puerto Rico.
1903	Treaty with Cuba signed embodying the Platt Amendment. Treaty with Panama creates the Canal Zone, and construction of the canal begins.
1904	Roosevelt Corollary to the Monroe Doctrine announced.
1905	Customs receivership established for the Dominican Republic.
1906–1909	United States intervenes in Cuba a second time, establishes military government there.
1912	Marines land in Cuba during the "Race War."
1915	United States occupies Haiti, establishes military government there.
1916	United States occupies the Dominican Republic, establishes military government there.
1917	U.S. Marines land in Cuba to protect mines, railroads, and sugar plantations; Jones Act gives Puerto Ricans U.S. citizenship.
1922	U.S. Marines leave Cuba.
1924	U.S. Marines leave the Dominican Republic.

1934	Platt Amendment revoked except for Guantanamo Bay lease; Jones-Costigan Act establishes a sugar marketing system, and Cuba receives a guaranteed annual quota; last U.S. Marines leave Haiti.
1940	United States signs Destroyer-for-Bases agreement with Great Britain; Act of Havana declares no transfer of European colonies in Caribbean; Dominican customs receivership ends.
1942	Anglo-American Caribbean Commission established.
1950	PL 600 replaces earlier governmental acts for Puerto Rico; Puerto Rican terrorists attempt to assassinate President Harry S. Truman.
1952	New constitution creates commonwealth status for Puerto Rico.
1954	Four Puerto Rican terrorists open fire on U.S. Congress.
1959	Fidel Castro comes to power in Cuba.
1961	United States breaks relations with Cuba; Bay of Pigs invasion attempt fails.
1962	Cuban missile crisis.
1964	U.S. intervention in the Dominican Republic.
1983	Caribbean Basin Initiative established; United States invades Grenada.
1989	United States invades Panama to oust General Manuel Noriega; President George Bush calls for vote on status of Puerto Rico.
1991	Caribbean Basin Initiative becomes permanent.

NOTES AND REFERENCES

PREFACE

1. Henry L. Stimson, *The United States and the Other American Republics*, Department of State, Latin American Series No. 4 (Washington, D.C.: U.S. Government Printing Office, 1931).

2. Secretary of State John Quincy Adams to Hugh Nelson, minister to Spain, 28 April 1823, in Worthington C. Ford, ed., *The Writings of John Quincy Adams* (New York: Macmillan, 1913–17), 7: 372–79.

3. Anthony Lake, *Somoza Falling* (Boston: Houghton-Mifflin, 1989), 58–59.

4. Thomas Paine, "Thoughts on Defensive War" (1775), quoted in Stephen P. Halbrook, *That Every Man Be Armed: The Evolution of a Constitutional Right* (Oakland, Calif.: The Independent Institute, 1984), 63.

CHAPTER 1

1. Thomas Fleming, "Hammering Havana's Walls," *Military History* (June 1987): 19–22.

2. Ibid.

3. Quoted in, Page Smith, *John Adams*, vol. 1, 1735–84 (Garden City, N.Y.: Doubleday, 1962), 567–68.

4. Michael A. Palmer, "Anglo-American Naval Cooperation, 1798–1801," *Naval History* (Summer 1990): 14–20.

5. Ibid.

6. Merrill D. Peterson, ed., *The Portable Thomas Jefferson* (New York: Viking Press, 1975), 486.

7. Secretary of State John Quincy Adams to Hugh Nelson (minister to Spain), 28 April 1823, in *The Writings of John Quincy Adams*, 7:372–79.

8. Robert L. O'Connell, "Post Haste," *American Heritage*, September–October 1989, 76–81.

9. *A Compilation of the Messages and Papers of the Presidents*, vol. 13 (New York: Bureau of National Literature, 1922), 6292.

10. Wood to Roosevelt, 28 October 1901, Box 29, Leonard Wood Papers, Library of Congress, Washington, D.C.

11. Ibid.

12. Holger M. Herwig, *Politics of Frustration: The United States in German Naval Planning, 1889–1941* (Boston: Little, Brown, 1976), 68–72.

13. Kaiser quoted in Holger M. Herwig, *Germany's Vision of Empire in Venezuela, 1871–1914* (Princeton, N.J.: Princeton University Press, 1986), 161; Herwig, *Politics*, 105.

14. Quoted in Thomas A. Bailey, *A Diplomatic History of the American People*, 9th ed. (Englewood Cliffs, N.J.: Prentice-Hall, 1974), 502.

15. Quoted in Allan Reed Millett, *The Politics of Intervention: The American Occupation of Cuba, 1906–1908* (Columbus: Ohio State University Press, 1968), 251.

16. *New York World*, 16 July 1916.

17. Memorandum, "Present Nature and Extent of the Monroe Doctrine," 24 November 1915, file 710.11/188, RG 59, Department of State, National Archives, Washington, D.C. Hereafter cited as SD and by file number.

18. CBS Television presentation, "World Wide 60": "Trujillo: Portrait of a Dictator," 10 March 1960.

19. Bowers to Roosevelt, 20 November 1944, and Roosevelt to Bowers, 20 December 1944, Franklin D. Roosevelt Papers, Franklin D. Roosevelt Library, Hyde Park, N.Y.; PSF File, box 36.

20. Welles to Roosevelt, 3 June 1940, Roosevelt MSS., PSF File, box 96; memorandum, "Hemisphere Defense," 11 June 1940, Latin American Affairs File, box 311; Harry Hopkins Papers, Roosevelt Library.

21. Brigadier General L. T. Gerow (acting chief of staff), Diary, 28 May–6 September 1941, OPD Executive File 1940–45, RG 165, Modern Military Division, National Archives, Washington, D.C. Hereafter cited as MMD. These bases were all returned shortly after the end of the war.

22. Lester D. Langley, *The United States and the Caribbean, 1900–1970* (Athens: University of Georgia Press, 1980), 178.

23. Joseph M. Jones, "Caribbean Laboratory: There We Can Learn the Potentials of U.S. Influence on World Colonial Policy," *Fortune*, February 1944, 126.

24. Ibid., 125.

25. Ibid. Charles W. Taussig to President Roosevelt, 22 April 1942; OF 4630, Roosevelt MSS.

26. For British attitudes and views, see memorandum of luncheon with Winston Churchill, 17 December 1942, Charles W. Taussig Papers, Roosevelt Library, file 1941–43 inclusive, box 52; memorandum, Lord Cranborne to Anthony Eden, 16 September 1942, Foreign Office of Great Britain, FO 371, file 30718, Public Records Office, London, England. Hereafter cited as PRO.

CHAPTER 2

1. Nelson Rockefeller Oral History, 639–40. A copy of this manuscript was sent to the author by the governor's staff.

2. George F. Kennan to Secretary Robert Lovett, 24 February 1948; Records of the Policy Planning Staff, 1947–55; General Records of the Department of State, RG 59.

3. Irwin R. Gellman, "Ruining Welles," paper presented at the seventeenth Annual Meeting of the Society for Historians of American Foreign Relations (1991). Rockefeller Oral History, 520–21.

4. Rockefeller Oral History, 624–25.

5. Berle to Fletcher Warren, 10 September 1945, Adolph A. Berle, Jr., Papers, Roosevelt Library.

6. Memorandum of 12 February 1946, memoranda on Nicaragua, vol. 3, box 52, Office of American Republic Affairs, 1918–47, SD.

7. 710.11/11-144, SD; Spruille Braden to Claude Bowers, 29 August 1946, 825.00/8-2956, SD.

8. Braden to Berle, 15 July 1945, 832.00/7-2545, SD. Bowers to Braden, 5 August 1946, 825.00/8-546, SD.

9. Note of 31 March 1945 by Mr. Cochran concerning Colonel Irving A. Lindberg; memoranda on Nicaragua, vol. 3, box 52, Office of American Republic Affairs, 1918–47, SD.

10. Joseph Grew to President Harry S. Truman, 2 May 1945, White House Central Files, confidential file, box 32, correspondence 1945 #1, Harry S. Truman Papers, Harry S. Truman Library (Independence, Mo.); "Relations of Caribbean Defense Command with Argentina" (no date, probably 1946), War Department Records, CMH Historical MSS., 1940–66, box 405; RG 319, MMD.

11. Ernest Bevin (British Foreign Office) to James F. Byrnes, 14 January 1946, 810.20 Defense/ 1-1446, SD; memorandum, "Arms and Munition to the Dominican Republic," by W. F. Barber for Cochran, Briggs, and Braden, 9 November 1945, 810.24/11-945 SD.

12. Memorandum for the president from the secretary of state, "President Somoza of Nicaragua," 3 September 1946, President's Secretary's File (PSF), subject file: Cabinet, box 159, Truman MSS.

13. Memorandum for the president from the secretary of state, "Recommendations Regarding Renewed Attempt of President Trujillo to Circumvent Policy" (nd), PSF, subject file: Foreign Affairs-Dominican Republic, box 176, Truman MSS.

14. Memorandum by the chief of the Division of Caribbean and Central American Affairs (Cochran), 3 June 1946, 815.248/5-2846 SD.

15. Memorandum from Braden to the secretary of state, "Latin American Arms Program," 16 December 1946, 810.24/12-1646 SD; Daniel M. Braddock to Ambassador William D. Pawley (Brazil), 27 December 1946, 810.24/12-2746 SD; memorandum by Dreier, "Comments on Military and Naval Objectives in the Other American Republics," 13 March 1945, 810.24/d3-1445 SD.

16. Memorandum for the chief of staff, "Latin American Background for Discussion with Mr. Acheson by General K. F. Hertford [chief, Pan-American Group, Operations and Planning Division, War Department General Staff]," 22 April 1946; P & O (1946–48), 400 Latin America, Case 2(5), War Department, Plans and Operations Division, RG 165, MMD; R. H. Hadow to T. Shuckburgh, 23 June 1947, FO 371, AS 3908, PRO.

17. Acheson to G. E. Savage, 8 April 1947, 710.11/4-847, SD.

18. Memorandum, "Agenda for Washington," 20 January 1945, 837.00/1-2045, SD.

19. 810.00/9-2746 SD.

20. Records of the Policy Planning Staff 1947–1953, 22 March 1948, Box 4; RG 59, SD.

21. Ibid.

22. "A Report to the National Security Council by the Department of State on U.S. Policy Regarding Anti-Communist Measures Which Could Be Planned and Carried Out within the Inter-American System," 28 June 1948 (NSC 16), PSF, Truman MSS.

23. Memorandum for the ambassador, 4 December 1946; George S. Messersmith Papers, University of Delaware Library (Newark); memorandum, "Ground Arms Purchases by Latin American Countries," 15 October 1948; MIS Project No. 4512, War Department Plans and Operations Division, P & O 1946–48, 400 Latin America, Case 69 (2), MMD.

24. Memorandum, "Trade in Armaments with the Latin American Countries," E. Bevin to representatives in Latin America, 20 March 1947, FO 371, AS 1271, PRO; memorandum for the secretary of state, 7 January 1947, FO 371, AS 247, PRO.

25. Ibid.

26. Memorandum, Attlee to Foreign Office, FO 371, AS 2045, PRO.

27. Minutes of cabinet meeting, 19 May 1947, FO 371, AS 3025; aide memoire left with the U.S. secretary of state, 30 April 1947, FO 371, AS 2705, PRO; memorandum, "Conversation between Lord Inverchapel [ambassador, Great Britain] and U.S. Secretary of State," 6 May 1947, 810.24/4-3047, SD.

28. Memorandum, "Timing of Announcements to Dominican Ambassador on Arms Decision," by Willard F. Barber (chief, Division of Caribbean Affairs), 31 July 1947; memoranda, Office of American Republics Affairs, 1918–47, box 13, SD.

29. Defense Department, "Draft of Order of Priority of Countries for Allocation of Spaces for Training of Foreign Nationals at U.S. Service Schools [other than academies]," 14 September 1949, 810.24/9-1449, SD.

30. Hand-written note from General Harry Vaughn to the president, 7 April 1952, PSF, subject file: Nicaragua, box 183, Truman MSS.

31. Miller to Thomas E. Whelan (ambassador to Nicaragua) 28 July 1952, box 3, Edward G. Miller Papers, Truman Library.

32. Memorandum, "A Year of 'Reconversion' in Our Cuban Relations," 12 September 1946, 711.37/9-1246, SD.

33. Memorandum for the president from Secretary of State Dean Acheson, 24 March 1952, confidential file, correspondence 1952, box 33 (file 30) Truman MSS.

34. Roosevelt to Tugwell, 7 November 1941, Rexford Guy Tugwell Papers, box 11, Roosevelt Library.

35. Tugwell to Roosevelt, 3 February 1942, box 11, Tugwell MSS.

36. Memorandum by Charles W. Taussig of a conversation with President Roosevelt, 15 March 1945, box 152, Charles W. Taussig Papers, Roosevelt Library.

37. FDR to Tugwell, 3 February 1942, box 11, Tugwell MSS.

38. Ickes to Bell, 1 November 1943, box 6, Tugwell MSS.; Tugwell to Bell, 14 October 1943, ibid.

39. Tugwell Diary, entry of 23 August 1945, box 19, Tugwell MSS; memorandum of conversation between President Truman and Charles W. Taussig, 8 January 1946, box 53, Taussig MSS.; Truman to Tugwell, 24 February 1946, box 13, Tugwell MSS.

40. Roland I. Perusse, *The United States and Puerto Rico: The Struggle for Equality* (Malabar, Fla.: Robert E. Krieger Publishing, 1990), 36.

41. Raymond Carr, *Puerto Rico: A Colonial Experiment* (New York: Vintage Books, 1984), 75.

CHAPTER 3

1. *Congressional Record*, vol. 98, pt. 8, 1952, A1316 (Mansfield).

2. "Latin America and U.S. Policy," sent in Thomas C. Mann to Charles S. Murphy, 11 December 1952, PSF, Truman MSS.

3. Rolando Bonachea and Nelson P. Valdes, *Revolutionary Struggle, 1947–1958* (Cambridge, Mass.: MIT Press, 1972), 1: 231, 379.

4. Herbert S. Dinerstein, *The Making of a Missile Crisis: October 1962* (Baltimore: Johns Hopkins University Press, 1976), 82–91.

5. Taylor Branch and George Crile III, "The Kennedy Vendetta: How the CIA Waged a Silent War against Cuba," *Harpers*, August 1975, 61.

6. Raymond L. Garthoff, *Reflections on the Cuban Missile Crisis*, rev. ed. (Washington, D.C.: Brookings Institution, 1989), 35–36.

7. Robert F. Kennedy, *Thirteen Days: A Memoir of the Cuban Missile Crisis* (New York: Signet Books, 1969), 31.

8.　Toledo, Ohio, *Blade*, 7 January 1992, 1. Article on heretofore undisclosed letters that were uncovered by Professor Philip Brenner.

9.　Joseph B. Smith, *Portrait of a Cold Warrior* (New York: Putnam, 1976), 377.

10.　Jerome Levinson and Juan de Onis, *The Alliance That Lost Its Way: A Critical Report of the Alliance for Progress* (Chicago: University of Chicago Press, 1970), 335–39.

11.　Ibid., 66.

12.　General Bruce Palmer, Jr., *Intervention in the Caribbean: The Dominican Crisis of 1965* (Lexington: University of Kentucky Press, 1989), 5. The United States suffered 350 casualties, including 44 killed.

13.　David Halberstam, "Lyndon," *Esquire*, August 1972, 79.

14.　Palmer, *Intervention*, 122.

15.　Minutes of cabinet meeting, 11 March 1955, Cabinet Series, Dwight D. Eisenhower Papers, Dwight D. Eisenhower Library (Abilene, Kans.).

CHAPTER 4

1.　Captain Leslie K. Fenlon, Jr., "The Umteenth Cuban Confrontation," *United States Naval Institute Proceedings* (July 1980): 44–45. Garthoff, *Reflections*, 145–46.

2.　Ensign Christopher A. Abel, "A Breach in the Ramparts," *United States Naval Institute Proceedings* (July 1980): 47–50.

3.　*Latin America* [London], 1 March 1974, 2.

4.　Arkady N. Shevchenko, *Breaking with Moscow* (New York: Alfred A. Knopf, 1985), 272, 262.

5.　Georgie Ann Geyer, *Guerrilla Prince: The Untold Story of Fidel Castro* (New York: Little, Brown, 1991), 354; John Norton Moore, *The Secret War in Central America: Sandinista Assault on World Order* (Frederick, Md.: University Publications of America, 1987), 10–11.

6.　"Nicaragua: U.S. Policy," *Gist* (a publication of the Bureau of Public Affairs of the U.S. Department of State), September 1979.

7.　Timothy Ashby, "Nicaragua: Soviet Satrapy," *United States Naval Institute Proceedings* (July 1984): 48–53; Mark Falcoff, "Cuba: First among Equals," in Dennis L. Bark, ed., *The Red Orchestra: Instruments of Soviet Policy in Latin America and the Caribbean* (Stanford, Calif.: Hoover Institution Press, 1986), 78–79; Andres Oppenheimer, *Castro's Final Hour: The Secret Story behind the Coming Downfall of Communist Cuba* (New York: Simon & Schuster, 1992), 195–96.

8.　Michael Novak, "Not So Simple El Salvador," *National Review*, 1 June 1984, 40; R. Bruce McColm, *El Salvador: Peaceful Revolution or Armed Struggle?* (New York: Freedom House, 1981), 38–41.

9.　"Eur Kampf," *National Review*, 3 April 1981, 335–36.

10.　McColm, *Peaceful Revolution or Armed Struggle?*, 26; Geyer, *Guerrilla Prince*, 359–60.

11. Jiri Valenta, "Soviet Strategy in the Caribbean Basin," *United States Naval Institute Proceedings* (May 1982): 178.

12. Geyer, *Castro*, 363–66.

13. U.S. Departments of State and Defense, *Grenada: A Preliminary Report* (Washington, D.C.: U.S. Government Printing Office, 1983), 30.

14. Memorandum by W. Richard Jacobs for Minister Unison Whiteman, Deputy Prime Minister Bernard Coard, and Ewart Layne, 11 July 1983, in Paul Seabury and Walter McDougall, eds., *The Grenada Papers* (San Francisco: Institute for Contemporary Studies, 1984), 207–8.

15. Geyer, *Castro*, 366.

16. Ibid.

17. *Grenada Papers*, 189–92.

18. Timothy Ashby, "Grenada: Soviet Stepping Stone," *United States Naval Institute Proceedings* (December 1983): 33–35.

19. Geyer, *Castro*, 372.

20. Ashby, "Grenada," 34.

21. Langhorne Motley (assistant secretary of state for inter-American affairs), "The Decision to Assist Grenada," U.S. Department of State, Bureau of Public Affairs, *Current Policy No. 541* (Washington, D.C.: U.S. Government Printing Office, 1984), 3.

22. Richard A. Gabriel, *Military Incompetence: Why the American Military Doesn't Win* (New York: Hill & Wang, 1985), 156–79.

23. Reynold A. Burrowes, *Revolution and Rescue in Grenada: An Account of the U.S.-Caribbean Invasion* (Westport, Conn.: Greenwood Press, 1988), 82–83.

24. Gabriel, *Military Incompetence*, 181–83.

25. Geyer, *Castro*, 377–78.

26. Ibid., 376–77.

27. Dennis Mullin, "Message from Grenada: 'Yankees Don't Go Home,'" *U.S. News & World Report*, 21 November 1983, 34.

28. Burrowes, *Revolution and Rescue*, 103, 114–15; Robert Masello, "Grenada," *Diversion* March 1989, 158.

29. "Grenada Story a Favorite in Ronald Reagan's Repertoire," *Armed Forces Journal*, April 1984, 85.

30. Stephen Kinzer, "Soviet Is Aiding Nicaragua in Buildup, Defector Says," *New York Times*, 14 December 1987, 1, 6.

31. Richard Perle, "America's Failure of Nerve," *U.S. News & World Report*, 10 August 1987, 32.

32. Ibid.

33. Kinzer, "Soviet Is Aiding," 1, 6.

34. Letter in *Commentary*, November 1991.

35. Artruro Cruz, Jr., "Family Feud Takes over Revolution," *Insight*, 25 February 1991, 36.

36. *Insight*, 4 March 1991, 30.

37. Linda Robinson, "A Last Bastion of Communism Gets a Little Lonelier," *U.S. News & World Report*, 23 September 1991, 44.

38. Toledo, Ohio, *Blade*, 19 September 1993, 3.

39. Letter from Nina Shea of the Puebla Institute, 13 December 1991.

40. Toledo, Ohio, *Blade*, 9 October 1993, 1.

41. Toledo, Ohio, *Blade*, 16 October 1993, 1.

42. Quoted in Langley, *Banana Wars*, 159. The Benet gun was a machine gun.

43. Carr, *Puerto Rico*, 348–63.

44. Perusse, *United States and Puerto Rico*, 52–53.

45. Christopher Caldwell, "Drive for Statehood Gains Momentum," *Insight*, 5 February 1990, 18–20.

46. Paul Glastris, "Pain Relief," *U.S. News & World Report*, 1 July 1991, 16.

47. Peter D. Whitney, "The CBI: Important Incentives for Trade and Investment," U.S. Department of State, Bureau of Public Affairs, *Current Policy No. 1065* (Washington, D.C.: U.S. Government Printing Office, 1988).

48. Peter D. Whitney, "Five Years of the Caribbean Basin Initiative," U.S. Department of State, Bureau of Public Affairs, *Current Policy No. 1241* (Washington, D.C.: U.S. Government Printing Office, 1989).

49. P.T. Bauer, "Western Guilt and Third World Poverty," *Commentary*, January 1976, 34.

CHAPTER 5

1. Carr, *Puerto Rico*, 294–95.

2. Frederick Pike, "Corporatism and Latin American–United States Relations," in Frederick Pike and Thomas Stritch, eds., *The New Corporatism: Social-Political Structures in the Iberian World* (Notre Dame, Ind.: University of Notre Dame Press, 1974), 138–39.

3. Eric Felten, "Love or Hate It, America is King of Pop Culture," *Insight*, 25 March 1991, 15.

4. Ernesto Cardenal, *In Cuba*, trans. Donald D. Walsh (New York: New Directions, 1974), 7, 115.

5. Carlos Alberto Motaner, "The Roots of Anti-Americanism in Cuba: Sovereignty in an Age of World Cultural Homogeneity," *Caribbean Review* (Spring 1984): 15–16, 44–45.

6. S. W. Bennett, album liner notes, Louis Moreau Gottschalk, *A Night in the Tropics* (New York: Vanguard Stereolab).

7. Philippe Rault, album liner notes, *Professor Longhair: Rock 'n' Roll Gumbo* (Santa Cruz, Calif.: Dancing Cat Records, 1985).

8. Perez, *Cuba and the United States*, 71–72.

9. Toledo, Ohio, *Blade*, 15 August 1991, 15.

10. Milton Jamail, "The Latin Market," *USA Today Baseball Weekly*, 9–15 August 1991, 50.

11. Ibid., 15.

12. Howard Means, *Colin Powell: A Biography* (New York: Ballantine Books, 1992), 57.

13. Diana West, "Cuban Exiles Rekindle Fire as Castro Inevitably Chills," *Insight*, 30 April 1990, 18–20.

14. Quoted in Lewis Gann and Peter Duignan, *The Hispanics in the United States: A History* (Boulder, Colo.: Westview Press, 1986), 111.

15. Gordon Witkin, Muadi Mukenge, et al., "The Men Who Created Crack," *U.S. News & World Report*, 19 August 1991, 44–53.

16. Rob Ruck, *The Tropic of Baseball: Baseball in the Dominican Republic* (Westport, Conn.: Meckler Press, 1991), 102.

CONCLUSION

1. Roger W. Fontaine, *On Negotiating with Cuba* (Washington, D.C.: American Enterprise Institute for Public Policy Research, 1975), 95.

2. U.S. Department of State, *The Atlantic Alliance* (Washington, D.C.: U.S. Government Printing Office, 1991), 31.

BIBLIOGRAPHIC ESSAY

For a most detailed presentation of U.S. relations with Latin America, see Graham Stuart and James Tigner, *Latin America and the United States*, 6th. ed. (Englewood Cliffs, N. J.: Prentice-Hall, 1975. Wilfrid Hardy Callcott's *The Western Hemisphere: Its Influence on United States Policies to the End of World War II* (Austin: University of Texas Press, 1968) is a well-balanced account of hemispheric relations and the international context. For a succinct, yet up-to-date and readable history of the Caribbean see Jan Rogozinski, *A Brief History of the Caribbean from the Arawak and the Carib to the Present* (New York: Facts on File, 1992).

The basic study of the Monroe Doctrine remains Dexter Perkins, *A History of the Monroe Doctrine*, rev. ed. (Boston: Houghton Mifflin, 1963). A related principle of U.S. diplomacy is fully discussed in John Logan, *No Transfer: An American Security Principle* (New Haven, Conn.: Yale University Press, 1961). A very useful introduction to Anglo-Spanish rivalry is J. Leitch Wright, *Anglo-Spanish Rivalry in North America* (Athens: University of Georgia Press, 1971). Two excellent works on eighteenth-century conflicts and commerce are Sir Richard Pares, *War and Trade in the West Indies, 1739–1763*, rep. ed. (London: P. Cass, 1963), and *Yankees and Creoles: The Trade between North America and the West Indies before the American Revolution*, rep. ed. (Hamden, Conn.: Archon Books, 1968).

A fine account of the British efforts to take Havana can be found in Thomas Fleming, "Hammering Havana's Walls," *Military History* (June 1987): 19–23. For the Caribbean dimension of the American Revolution see James A. Lewis, *The Final Campaign of the American Revolution: Rise and Fall of the Spanish Bahamas* (Columbia: University of South Carolina Press, 1991). For the best account of the subject see Michael A. Palmer, "Anglo-American Naval Cooperation, 1798–1801," *Naval History* (Summer 1990): 14–20. For commercial problems after the War for Independence consult Vernon G. Setser, *The Commercial Reciprocity Policy of the United States, 1774–1829* (Philadelphia: University of Pennsylvania Press, 1937), and Benjamin H. Williams, *Economic Foreign Policy of the United States* (New York: McGraw-Hill, 1929). The Setser volume is indispensable for any understanding of trade problems since almost nothing has been written since.

A useful introduction is Lester D. Langley *Struggle for the American Mediterranean: United States-European Rivalry in the Gulf-Caribbean, 1776–1904* (Athens: University of Georgia Press, 1976). The British position in the nineteenth century is given excellent coverage in several essays of R. A. Humphreys, *Tradition and Revolt in Latin America and Other Essays* (New York: Columbia University Press, 1969), and Mary Wilhelmine Williams, *Anglo-American Isthmian Diplomacy, 1815–1915* (Washington, D.C.: American Historical Association, 1916). The role of agents and adventurers in extending U.S. interests is described in Roy F. Nichols, *Advance Agents of American Destiny* (Philadelphia: University of Pennsylvania Press, 1956). The most detailed and scholarly study for one island is Charles Callan Tansill, *The United States and Santo Domingo, 1798–1873* (Baltimore: Johns Hopkins University Press, 1938). Similar is Rayford Logan, *The Diplomatic Relations of the United States with Haiti, 1776–1891* (Chapel Hill: University of North Carolina Press, 1941). The important impact that events in Haiti had on the southern United States is presented in Alfred N. Hunt, *Haiti's Influence on Antebellum America: Slumbering Volcano in the Caribbean* (Baton Rouge: Louisiana State University Press, 1992). A fine analysis of the South's role in U.S. involvement in the Caribbean before the Civil War is Robert May, *The Southern Dream of a Caribbean Empire, 1854–1861* (Baton Rouge: Louisiana State University Press, 1973).

For the expansionism of the latter part of the nineteenth century and the emergence of the United States as a world power see two excellent studies: H. Wayne Morgan, *America's Road to Empire: The War with Spain and Overseas Expansion* (New York: John Wiley & Sons, 1965) and David Healy, *U.S. Expansionism: the Imperialist Urge in the 1890s* (Madison: University of Wisconsin Press, 1970). An old but still useful study is Julius W. Pratt, *Expansionists of 1898: The Acquisition of Hawaii and the Spanish Islands* (Baltimore: Johns Hopkins University Press, 1936). For the religious foundations of American actions, see Robert Freeman Smith, "Protestant Millenarianism and United States Foreign Relations at the End of the Nineteenth Century," *Hayes Historical Journal* (Summer 1990):24–35.

The history of U.S. relations with Cuba is covered in Hugh Thomas's very detailed study, *Cuba: The Pursuit of Freedom* (New York: Harper & Row, 1971). More compact and critical of the U.S. is Louis A. Perez, Jr., *Cuba and the United States: Ties of Singular Intimacy* (Athens: University of Georgia Press, 1990). A different approach that combines narrative with documents is Robert Freeman Smith, *What Happened in Cuba? A Documentary History* (New York: Twayne Publishers, 1963). A Marxist-Leninist view of the U.S. involvement in Cuba is Philip Foner, *The Spanish-Cuban-American War and the Birth of American Imperialism*, 2 vols. (New York: Monthly Review Press, 1972). A much more balanced analysis is David Healy, *The United States in Cuba, 1898–1902: Generals, Politicians, and the Search for Policy* (Madison: University of Wisconsin Press, 1963). A fine study of the second intervention is Allan Reed Millett, *The Politics of Intervention: The Military Occupation of Cuba, 1906–1909* (Columbus: Ohio State University Press, 1968). A detailed analysis of U.S. policy and Cuban politics is Louis A. Perez, Jr., *Intervention, Revolution, and Politics in Cuba, 1913–1921* (Pittsburgh: University of Pittsburgh Press, 1978). A study that forces events into the dependency-theory mold is Jules Benjamin, *The United States and Cuba: Hegemony and Dependent Development, 1880–1934* (Pittsburgh: University of Pittsburgh Press, 1974).

For detailed analyses of the European role in the twentieth century see Warren Kneer, *Great Britain and the Caribbean, 1901–1913* (East Lansing: Michigan State University Press, 1975), and Sir Harold Mitchell, *Europe in the Caribbean: The Policies of Great Britain, France, and the Netherlands towards Their West Indian Territories in the Twentieth Century* (Stanford, Calif.: Hispanic American Society, 1963). A first-rate study of German imperial ambitions can be found in Holger H. Herwig, *Germany's Vision of Empire in Venezuela, 1871–1914* (Princeton, N.J.: Princeton University Press, 1986).

The best and most balanced analysis of the U.S. role in the Caribbean in the early part of the twentieth century is David Healy, *Drive to Hegemony: the United States in the Caribbean, 1898–1917* (Madison: University of Wisconsin Press, 1988). Healy sets the

Caribbean policy of the United States in the broader context of international relations. Lester D. Langley's *The United States in the Caribbean, 1900–1970* (Athens: University of Georgia Press, 1980) blames most of the area's ills on the United States, but his *The Banana Wars: An Inner History of American Empire, 1900–1934* (Lexington: University of Kentucky Press, 1983) provides a fascinating and more balanced view of the military elements of American intervention. Ivan Musicant, *The Banana Wars: A History of United States Military Interventions in Latin America from the Spanish-American War to the Invasion of Panama* (New York: Macmillan, 1990), is a broader coverage of the same topic and a well-written and authoritative survey. The most detailed coverage of the subject is Donald A. Yerxa, "The United States Navy in Caribbean Waters during World War I," *Military Affairs* (October 1987):182–87.

Studies emphasizing strategic factors are Dana Munro, *Intervention and Dollar Diplomacy in the Caribbean, 1900–1921* (Princeton, N.J.: Princeton University Press, 1964) and *The U.S. and the Caribbean Republics, 1921–1933* (Princeton, N.J.: Princeton University Press, 1974). Wilfrid Hardy Callcott's *The Caribbean Policy of the United States, 1890–1920* (Baltimore: Johns Hopkins University Press, 1942) is a dated but still useful introduction emphasizing the role of the canal on U.S. policy. Much the same can be said for Howard C. Hill, *Roosevelt and the Caribbean* (Chicago: University of Chicago Press, 1927). An extensively researched and insightful study using the international context as well as the domestic political contexts of the U.S. and the Caribbean is Richard H. Collin, *Theodore Roosevelt's Caribbean: The Panama Canal, the Monroe Doctrine, and the Latin American Context* (Baton Rouge: Louisiana State University Press, 1990).

Hans Schmidt, *The United States Occupation of Haiti, 1915–1934* (New Brunswick, N.J.: Rutgers University Press, 1971), stresses racist and cultural factors and is most critical of the United States. A well-balanced presentation of the same situation is David Healy, *Gunboat Diplomacy in the Wilson Era: The United States in Haiti, 1915–1916* (Madison: University of Wisconsin Press, 1976). I discuss the role of business in U.S.-Cuban relations in *The United States and Cuba: Business and Diplomacy, 1917–1960* (New York: Bookman Associates, 1960). For a good study analyzing the way the Republicans altered U.S. policy, see Kenneth J. Grieb, *The Latin American Policy of Warren G. Harding* (Fort Worth: Texas Christian University Press, 1976). The official view of the Marine occupation of the Dominican Republic is Captain Stephen M. Fuller and Graham A. Cosmas, *Marines in the Dominican Republic, 1916–1924* (Washington, D.C.: History and Museums Division, U.S. Marine Corps Headquarters, 1974). For a detailed study of the foundation of national guards in the Dominican Republic and Nicaragua consult Marvin Goldwert, *The Constabulary in the Dominican Republic and Nicaragua: Progeny and Legacy of United States Intervention* (Gainesville: University of Florida Press, 1962).

One of the best studies of Good Neighbor diplomacy in the region is Irwin R. Gellman, *Batista and Roosevelt: Good Neighbor Diplomacy in Cuba, 1933–1945* (Albuquerque: University of New Mexico Press, 1973). For a well-documented study of the U.S. impact on the European colonies see Fitzroy André Baptiste, *War, Cooperation, and Conflict: The European Possessions in the Caribbean, 1939–1945* (Westport, Conn.: Greenwood Press, 1988). For Puerto Rico the standard work is Thomas Mathews, *Puerto Rican Politics and the New Deal* (Gainesville: University of Florida Press, 1960). A short but very useful introduction is Roland I. Perusse, *The United States and Puerto Rico: The Struggle for Equality* (Malabar, Fla.: Robert E. Krieger Publishing, 1990). Raymond Carr, *Puerto Rico: A Colonial Experiment* (New York: Vintage Books, 1984), is a more detailed and analytical account. This well-balanced study can be compared with an extremely critical work, Gordon Lewis, *Puerto Rico: Freedom and Power in the Caribbean* (New York: Harper & Row, 1963). The most authoritative study for the Dominican Republic is G. Pope Atkins and Larman C. Wilson, *The United States and the Trujillo Regime* (New Brunswick, N.J.: Rutgers University Press, 1972).

The post–World War II period is still something of a literary wasteland when one looks for good scholarly works. Too much of the literature is either current-eventy or highly ideological sermonizing. The Cuban revolution of Fidel Castro has produced a mountain of books on U.S. relations with the island. Most are best forgotten. The best starting point is Hugh Thomas, The Cuban Revolution (New York: Harper & Row, 1977), a shortened version of his Cuba: The Pursuit of Freedom. For a scholarly, balanced analysis of the early U.S. response see Richard Welch, Jr., Response to Revolution: The United States and the Cuban Revolution, 1959–1961 (Chapel Hill: University of North Carolina Press, 1985). Of special interest is the author's consideration of various nongovernmental responses. The best discussion of Castro's personality/ideology and its influence on relations with the United States is Georgie Anne Geyer, Guerrilla Prince: The Untold Story of Fidel Castro (Boston: Little, Brown, 1991). The interested reader must consult the volume by the U.S. ambassador to Cuba until relations were broken in 1960, Philip W. Bonsal, Cuba, Castro, and the United States (Pittsburgh: University of Pittsburgh Press, 1971). For a work that makes Castro and his revolution the inevitable products of U.S. chicanery and imperialism see Michael J. Mazarr, Semper Fidel: America and Cuba, 1776–1988 (Baltimore: Nautical and Aviation Publishing Company of America, 1988).

The two major crises in U.S.-Cuban relations during the post-1959 period have produced numerous works. Dated but still useful for some background information is Karl Meyer and Tad Szulc, The Cuban Invasion: The Chronicle of a Disaster (New York: Praeger, 1962). Two good analyses that draw on a wide range of sources are Peter Wyden, Bay of Pigs: The Untold Story (New York: Simon & Schuster, 1979), and Trumbull Higgins, The Perfect Failure: Kennedy, Eisenhower, and the CIA at the Bay of Pigs (New York: Norton, 1987). The latter concentrates on policy making and neglects the actual operational factors. For a most informative primary source, see General Maxwell Taylor's Board of Inquiry on Cuban Operations Conducted by the CIA, Operation Zapata: The "Ultrasensitive" Report and Testimony of the Board of Inquiry on the Bay of Pigs (Frederick, Md.: University Publications of America, 1981). For the Missile Crisis a good introduction can be found in Elie Abel, The Missile Crisis (Philadelphia: J. B. Lippincott, 1966), and Herbert S. Dinerstein, The Making of a Missile Crisis: October 1962 (Baltimore: Johns Hopkins University Press, 1976). Recent revelations by both the Cubans and the Soviets are found in Raymond L. Garthoff, Reflections on the Cuban Missile Crisis, rev. ed. (Washington, D.C.: Brookings Institution, 1989), and James G. Blight and David A. Welch, On the Brink: Americans and Soviets Reexamine the Cuban Missile Crisis (New York: Hill & Wang, 1989). An in-depth insider analysis is provided in Dino A. Brugioni, Eyeball to Eyeball: The Inside Story of the Cuban Missile Crisis (New York: Random House, 1992). The author, a CIA officer from 1948 to 1982, was chief of the photographic interpretation unit that actually prepared the crucial, aerial photographs for the White House during the Missile Crisis. Heretofore classified papers are published in, Central Intelligence Agency, The Secret Cuban Crisis Documents, New York: Brassey's (U.S.), 1993. The inside Soviet view is presented by the former Soviet official, Yuri Pavlov Soviet-Cuban Alliance, 1959–1991, Miami, Florida: University of Miami North-South Center Book, 1993.

For the U.S., European, and Cuban press and the Castro revolution see the excellent study by William E. Ratliff, ed., The Selling of Fidel Castro: The Media and the Cuban Revolution (New Brunswick, N.J.: Transaction Books, 1987). For Castro's involvement in the international drug trade, see Castro and the Narcotics Connection: The Cuban Government's Use of Narcotics Trafficking to Finance and Promote Terrorism (Washington, D.C.: Cuban American National Foundation, 1983). For detailed accounts of the Cuban involvement in Nicaragua consult Glenn Garvin, Everybody Had His Own Gringo: The CIA and the Contras (Washington, D.C.: Brassey Books, 1992), and Sam Dillon, Commandos: The CIA and Nicaragua's Contra Rebels (New York: Henry Holt, 1991). An excellent analysis of developments in Cuba from the latter 1980s is Andres Oppenheimer, *Castro's Final Hour: The Secret Story behind the Coming Downfall of Communist Cuba* (New York: Simon & Schuster, 1992), which is based on extensive work inside Cuba and contains important documentation for Castro's role in Central America and the Caribbean.

For the Dominican Intervention of 1965, two well-researched volumes are Lawrence A. Yates, *Power Pack: U.S. Intervention in the Dominican Republic, 1965–1966* (Leavenworth Papers No. 15., Fort Leavenworth, Kans.: U.S. Army Command and General Staff College, 1988), and Audrey Bracey, *Resolution of the Dominican Crisis, 1965: A Study in Mediation* (Washington, D.C.: Institute for the Study of Diplomacy, Edmund A. Walsh School of Foreign Service, Georgetown University, 1980). A very critical account of the U.S. action can be found in Piero Gleijeses, *The Dominican Crisis: The 1965 Constitutional Revolt and American Intervention* (Baltimore: Johns Hopkins University Press, 1978). For insightful analyses by participants see John Bartlow Martin, *Overtaken by Events* (New York: Doubleday, 1966), and General Bruce Palmer, Jr., *Intervention in the Caribbean: The Dominican Crisis of 1965* (Lexington: University of Kentucky Press, 1989).

Reynold A. Burrowes, *Revolution and Rescue in Grenada: An Account of the U.S.-Caribbean Invasion* (Westport, Conn.: Greenwood Press, 1988); Jiri Valenta and Herbert J. Ellison, eds., *Grenada and Soviet/Cuban Policy: Internal Crisis and U.S./IECS Intervention* (Boulder, Colo.: Westview Press, 1986); and Gregory Sanford and Richard Vigilante, *Grenada: The Untold Story* (Lanham, Md.: Madison Books, 1984) are good introductions to most aspects of the story. The latter two make good use of captured documents. Collections of captured documents are Paul Seabury and Walter McDougall, eds., *The Grenada Papers* (San Francisco: Institute for Comtemporary Affairs, 1984), and, U.S. Departments of State and Defense, *Grenada Documents: An Overview and Selection* (Washington, D.C.: U.S. Government Printing Office, 1984). A critical but honest evaluation of the military operations from a British perspective is Major Mark Adkins, *Urgent Fury: The Battle for Grenada* (Lexington, Mass.: Lexington Books, 1989). An anti-U.S. account can be found in Anthony Payne and Tony Thorndike, *Grenada: Revolution and Invasion.* (New York: St. Martin's, 1984).

One of the best analyses of the impact of Caribbean immigration on the United States is Lewis Gann and Peter Duignan, *The Hispanics in the United States: A History* (Boulder, Colo.: Westview Press, 1986). For two specific groups, see Alejandro Portes and Robert L. Bach, *Latin Journey: Cuban and Mexican Immigrants in the U.S.* (Berkeley: University of California Press, 1985); Damián J. Fernández, "From Little Havana to Washington, D.C.: The Impact of Cuban-Americans on U.S. Foreign Policy," in Mohammed Ahari, ed., *Ethnic Groups and Foreign Policy* (Westport, Conn.: Greenwood Press, 1987); and Joseph P. Fitzpatrick, *Puerto Rican Americans: The Meaning of Migration to the Mainland* (Englewood Cliffs, N.J.: Prentice-Hall, 1987). The real flavor of the role of baseball in the Dominican is analyzed in this spirited and carefully crafted account—Rob Ruck, *The Tropic of Baseball: Baseball in the Dominican Republic* (Westport, Conn.: Meckler Press, 1991). A much duller study from an anthropological angle is Alan M. Klein, *Sugarball: The American Game, the Dominican Dream* (New Haven, Conn.: Yale University Press, 1991).

Soviet strategy and tactics prior to the 1991 collapse is well developed in Dennis L. Bark, *The Red Orchestra: Instruments of Soviet Policy in Latin America and the Caribbean* (Stanford, Calif.: Hoover Institution Press, 1986). A collection of essays analyzing U.S. policy and Caribbean developments in the 1980s from various points of view is Mark Falcoff and Robert Royal, eds., *U.S. Policy in Central America and the Caribbean* (Lanham, Md.: Ethics and Public Policy Center, 1987). Unlike other anthologies, here the conservative position is given a fair shake.

INDEX

Acheson, Dean, 31
Act of Dominican Reconciliation, 50
Act of Havana concerning the
       Provisional Administration of
       European Colonies or
       Possessions in the Americas, 23
Adams, John, 2, 4
Adams, John Quincy, xiii–xiv, 5, 6
Afghanistan, Soviet invasion of, 58
Agency for International Development
       (AID), 48, 51, 67
Agnew, Spiro, 55
Alberto Montaner, Carlos, 85
Albizu Campos, Pedro, 35, 37, 38
Alliance for Progress, 47, 48, 51, 92–93
Alomar, Roberto, 88
Alomar, Sandy, Jr., 88
Alou, Felipe, 88
Alou, Jesus, 88
Alou, Mateo, 88
Anglo-American Caribbean
       Commission, 24
Angola, 54, 56, 66
Antigua, U.S. military bases in, 23
Arbenz, Jacobo, 40
Arenas, Reinaldo, 58
Arevalo, Marcos, 71
Argentina, 28, 30, 31, 32, 33
Arias, Oscar, 69
Aristide, Jean-Bertrand, 75, 76, 77
Aricha, René, 87

arms sales and transfers, 30–33, 40, 42,
       57–58, 60–62, 68–69
Aronson, Bernard, 72
Austin, Hudson, 64

Bahamas, 78, 89; U.S. military bases in,
       23
Balaguer, Joaquin, 50
Balfour, Arthur, 16
Barbados, 64, 65, 67
baseball, influence on culture of the
       Caribbean region, 87–88
Batista y Zaldívar, Fulgencio, 20, 21, 22,
       30, 34, 42
Bauer, P. T., 82–83
Bay of Pigs invasion, 44–45, 46, 89
Becquer, Julio, 87
Bell, C. Jasper, 36
Benitez, Jaime, 36
Berle, Adolf A., Jr., 28, 29
Bermuda, 5; U.S. military bases in, 23
Bidlack-Mallarino Treaty (Treaty of
       New Grenada), 6
Bishop, Maurice, 59, 60, 61, 62, 63
Black War Plan, 16
Black Warrior affair, 7
Boland Amendments, 67–68
Boland, Edward, 67
Bonaparte, Napoleon, 3, 4
Bonner, Robert, 74
Bonsal, Phillip, 42

THE AUTHOR

Robert Freeman Smith is professor of history at the University of Toledo. He received his B.A. and M.A. from the University of Arkansas and his Ph.D. from the University of Wisconsin. He has served on the faculties of the Universities of Arkansas, Wisconsin, Rhode Island, and Connecticut. His books include *The United States and Cuba: Business and Diplomacy, 1917–1960* (1960), which received the Texas Writer's Roundup Award in 1961; *The United States and Revolutionary Nationalism in Mexico, 1916–1932* (1972), which received the Ohio Academy of History book award in 1973; and *The United States and the Latin American Sphere of Influence: The Era of Good Neighbors, Cold Warriors, and Hairshirts* (1983).

Smith received the Truman Library's Tom L. Evans Research Fellowship in 1976 and in 1991 was invited by the Mexican Ministry of Foreign Relations to participate in a project dealing with the United States and the Mexican Revolution. He served in the U.S. Army during the Korean War and is currently a lieutenant colonel in the Ohio Military Reserve.

DATE DUE